Reflections On Being Human

- POEMS -

NIRANDER SAFAYA, Ph.D.

REFLECTIONS
on
BEING HUMAN

REFLECTIONS
—————on—————
BEING HUMAN

POEMS

Nirander Safaya, Ph.D.

ARPress
ILLUMINATING IDEAS.
EMPOWERING VOICES

ARPress
45 Dan Road Suite 5
Canton MA 02021

Hotline: 1(888) 821-0229
Fax: 1(508) 545-7580

Ordering Information:
Quantity sales. Special discounts are available on quantity purchases by corporations, associations, and others. For details, contact the publisher at the address above.

Printed in the United States of America.

ISBN-13:	Softcover	979-8-89356-704-5
	Hardcover	979-8-89356-705-2
	eBook	979-8-89356-706-9

Library of Congress Control Number: 2024904902

Contents

Part II: Reflections on Love

Part III: Reflections on Light

<u>Dedication</u>

To my children: Pushkin, Seema, and Rubin,
for teaching me unceasingly;

And

To my grandchildren: Alex, Ashley, Hunter, and Gia,
for watching the world innocently;

And

To my divine Muse
for graciously inspiring me.

Preface

Many people think that science and religion are incompatible and "never the twain shall meet." This feeling persists despite the fact that both of these domains endeavor to find *truth*. Both place full faith in their own methods and findings, whether they are based on a mathematical equation, scientific experimentation, intuition, spiritual revelation, or a hymn that touches the soul. In the same vein, poetry offers a unique medium to explore and express the truth and beauty of human nature and our aspirations for aesthetic and spiritual fulfillment.

Any attempt to bridge the gulf between the scientific and spiritual visions of humankind is useful. It leads us to discover and accept *truth* without compromising our faith in ourselves, our heritage, and the spirit and purpose that underlie our existence. Poets and philosophers have played a significant role in this process for centuries. Because of the inherent aesthetics and figurative power in poetry, its thought content is generally easier to digest than that of science or philosophy.

Having worked as a scientist for forty years, with an abiding interest in world literature, philosophy, and religions, I was tempted to paint some of the realities of life with the evocative brush of poetry. So, after my retirement, I began to write poems about life, love, and light to illustrate how our ordinary experiences lead to self-knowledge and some understanding of human and divine nature. I chose poetry because of its precision, as science has, and its appeal to feelings, as religion has. Besides, poetry leans on philosophy for its ethics and aesthetics.

In this collection of my poems, *Reflections on Being Human,* I have tried to catch some glimpses of the joys and sorrows of life and love, and the saving grace of light —all of which contribute to human experience and existence. I hope my readers will take some comfort in thinking that hard facts and soft feelings can coexist, and that our scientific and spiritual paths for discovering truth will eventually get closer. In the meantime we must continue enjoying life in all its multiple forms of art that deeply touch our *hearts*.

Nirander Safaya
Leander, TX. USA

Acknowledgements

My deepest gratitude goes to my late wife, Shama, and to our children – Seema, Pushkin and Rubin – for inspiring me to reflect and write about human condition: emotions, aspirations and behavior. Shama provided me the needed support and valuable suggestions during the development of my poetic work contained in this volume.

I am indebted to my brother, Dataji, for encouraging me to get my poems published. My thanks are also due to my sister, Sarla, and her husband, Dr. Mohan Wali; and to my esteemed friends: Dr. Steve Merrill, Dan Chris and Denny Wilshire for critiquing my poems. I also wish to thank all my professional reviewers and lay persons who have read and commented on my poetry with discerning and uplifting remarks.

Reflections On Being Human was first published by iUniverse in 2016. But now a special edition of the same book has been published by The Author Reputation Press (APR), on the loving insistence of their author advisor, Clint Stevenson. I thank him for his appreciative eye and sound judgement. I am also beholden to APR's book fulfillment officer, Astrid Whittman, for her prodigious patience, understanding, and encouragement. Finally, I wish to thank ARP's interior layout artist, Luke Garner, for designing the interior of this book.

Part I

Reflections on Life

Life

"The universe is change;
Our life is what our thoughts make it."
-Marcus Aurelius

"The calm circumference of life
When I would fain have kept,
Time caught me in the tide of strife
And to center swept."
-Hafez

Life

"What mortal, when he saw,
Life's voyage done, his heavenly Friend,
Could ever yet dare tell him fearlessly:
'I have kept uninfringed my nature's law;
The inly-written chart thou gavest me
To guide me, I have steer'd by to the end'?"
-Mathew Arnold, *Human Life*

Oh, I have yet to go a few miles more,
Make a few calls at this and that store,
And visit one more beckoning shore,
Lest I forget to pay what I owed before.
Let me finish this business, and nothing more.
Then I will see you.

In the budding spring of my youth,
I didn't look for the hidden truth,
For love and learning came naturally smooth.
All was arranged neatly in its assigned booth,
But without any sense of the missing truth.
Then did I think of you?

The glory of summer was no simple matter.
There were many desires to quench
And hungry passions to feed – sooner than later.
In these pursuits, there were some egos to flatter.
Right or wrong, success alone seemed to matter.
Then did I think of you?

As the summer peaked, new vanities grew,
Drawing attention to things I hardly knew;
For the glamour of power and position in society,
A fuzzy line between prowess and prudence I drew.
My passion for sham recognition demonically grew.
Then did I think of you?

Now, when I am old and in the season of fall,
The green in nature having turned gold,
A strong voice seems to beckon and persistently call,
Lifting its eye from books of yore, encompassing all
That matters most — dear God, I will not fail or fold.
Now I crave to see you.

The Journey

Childhood fancies make us grow,
Youth's urges keep us on the toe,
The prime of life tells us to sow
Seeds of trust — for love to grow.
Old age brings us a marvelous gift.
First, it does our many burdens lift:
We don't carry the same old ego,
For, with time, we grow mellow.

Each child comes with God's gift,
Given as parental love and genes
That determine our base and tilt,
Our raw nature and adaptive skills.
Thus nature and nurture combined
May shape us into a person divine
Or make us a creature of evil mind;
And each of these gives its own sign.

From early on we begin to explore
The world around and within us,
Feeding on knowledge and more,
Generally without too much fuss.
But soon our focus shifts to love
(First to the earthly, then divine)
That touches us gently from above,
Guiding us by its power sublime.

At each stage of our trenchant life,
We encounter some joy and strife;
Neither remains too long with us,
But we can't our feelings suppress.
All pursuits arise from love or hate;
These in turn determine our fate.
Of all the drivers, love is the best,
For it keeps us flying over the crest.

The Enchanted Hill

Step by step, arm in arm, we ascend the live hill.
Steep and rugged though it is, a passionate thrill
Keeps us going without rest, to test our restless will
And see the truth that lies behind the enchanted hill.

It is no ordinary hill of earth and rock and scrub,
Nor is it pointed skyward as a tall, tangible nub —
Challenging our muscles and sinews to grind or rub
Against its gritty side, without a shady tree or shrub.

The hill changes its shape with our each step,
And after each moment — which is surely kept
Stored in memory — it morphs, as it deems apt,
Into something quite unknown and out of step.

Out of step, and unlike its past reality and repose,
It assumes a shape nowhere reminiscent or close
To its former semblance or purpose, as we suppose,
But a new state of being — an altogether new repose.

Call it as you may, but look deeply into its mystery:
The hill morphs to test our memory of its history,
Written by us and the hill together in live chemistry,
Recounting trials, toils, gains, and mind's mastery.

The enchanted hill feeds on our feelings and flesh;
It teases and tortures and then restores us afresh,
Kindling hope and purpose in our weakened breast
Until we scale its last hurdle in one leap of trust.

Signs of Life

From the lay of this piece of land,
Long abandoned, one can see
That generations of men and women
Lived and labored here — hand in hand.

The cottages with terraced gardens
That once stood proudly on this hill,
Have all weathered and tumbled down
Time's silent slope without a frown.

A moving sense of form and beauty
In them who lived here is still visible
In the fallen arches and empty altars,
Dry fountains and sagging shelters.

But the air above the dirt and rubble
Is crisp and clear — like a new bell,
Still echoing with the songs and mirth
Poured here at each festival and birth.

The songs those men and women sang
Joyously with each other and with life
Must have been played in full tune
With the thrushes — welcoming June.

The sun and stars shine over this place
As before and seem to secretly know:
The life that was teaming here once
Hasn't been extinguished from thence.

A gentle breeze stirs the fallen leaves
On sunken roofs and the bare ground,
Like they want to come back to life;
For here, indeed, lust for life was rife.

I wonder: What happened to those
Who once vigorously thrived here!
Was it some grim disease or drought
Or just Time's ever-streaming rout!

Time is a persistent old gypsy man.
It bestows glories wherever it can,
Depending on people's will and skill;
Then leaves to nature its mission to fulfill.

A Measure of Life

We fill and empty our minds each day,
Like coffee cups, soup bowls, and plates,
And wash our memories down the drain,
Just to make our lives simple and plain.

We rearrange the cupboards and closets,
Blow out the dust, wipe away the grime,
And rinse our hands to wash away time –
Its huge burdens and obligations prime.

We comb the stores and the countryside
In search of things we assume we need:
Food and drink for body and mind aside,
Casual lovers, passions, and desires to feed.

Like Sisyphus, tied to the rock of routine,
We fill the hours with our labor and love,
While our mortal frames westward lean,
Yet our efforts seem worthwhile somehow.

This routine appears right, and aptly so,
For there, indeed, all the pleasures do meet
When love, labor, and laughter together go,
And one's daily life is just, simple, and sweet.

Horizon

If only I could reach the horizon and stand
Where the earth rises to embrace the sky,
I could catch the heaven's azure in my eye
And touch the silvery clouds floating by,
While my feet are planted on solid ground.

The horizon is distantly circled around me,
But as I walk toward it from any direction,
It recedes away at the same pace,
Leaving me at its center, even if I race.
So I wonder what a challenge I face!

I have been walking toward the horizon
All my life — without any success in sight,
Calling worldly commerce my delight,
Beguiling time in its cycles of day and night.
So confined, my life will surely fade away.

I believe I should keep on going, searching
A way out of the conundrum of life's longings,
Cast away attachments, beliefs, and belongings,
And begin again earnestly to brace my will
For ending the agonies of my own making.

But if my efforts to reach the horizon fall shy,
Then let it come to me on its own wings.
I am ready to receive it on the hills or dales,
Seething deserts or rough seas lashed by gales.
For I want to touch the horizon before I die.

A Measure of Time

Motion of bodies in space
Becomes *Time*,
As the moving hands of a clock
Or the beats of a pulsating heart,
Each jogging at its own pace,
None leaving a lasting trace.

Like an elastic string in a lace,
Time is a yarn in the fabric of space,
But without a recognizable face –
So much like mortal love,
Which comes into its being
Only when we are actually living.

We like to keep track of all events,
Even silly thoughts that come and go
Or the emotions that set us high or low.
But there is nothing that prevents
Time from its insensate flow
Through our fingers – fast or slow.

It is easier to invoke fate
Than to ask of *time* a favor:
To lead us away from the open gate
To perdition and God's disfavor.
For *time* has a cruel streak:
It turns us all old and weak.
So let us keep on moving,

At our own sweet pace going.
It isn't being early or late
That changes our fate,
But the labor of love
That gets rewarded somehow.

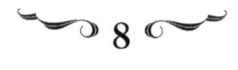
now

oh my love,
where shall i start?
in the mind or in heart!
the one is empty and still,
the other filled to the brim.
sorrow found a cozy place
in my heart's free space
and drained my mind
of its will to face,
oh, dear God,
my loss,
alas!
as i go
racing down
the memory lane,
searching through the
cold, ashy ruins of my past,
i find there nothing worthy
to ponder about or possess—
just a few scraps of rusted
metal buried in the soul.
then it comes to me:
i too had, once,
some grit
in me.
now as
i consider duly
the path i must take,
which may lie betwixt
that one of my choosing
or of destiny's own doing,
i should remold the ashes
of my past into a dense
block of gritty steel
fired in the fair
mercy and
will of God

Here and Now

I see now, it is the Here and Now
That beckon me most; not as how
Ego's impetuous brother, Id, tugs
Hard to enjoy the Dionysian drugs,

But to make up for the time lost
In remembrances that dearly cost
And future dreams that don't last.
So to Here and Now I hold fast.

The past is done; it can't be undone,
Not a line, dash, or dot made in fun
By wit or magic unwrit or erased—
This truth about Past must be faced.

Future flies in expanding space.
There infinite chances one shall face
In the changing reality of the world
Wherein we all are helplessly hurled.

Verily, Here and Now is that point
Where Past and Future are conjoint:
Past is a shadow that exists no more;
Future a phantom never seen before.

The present has a real, tangible form;
Revel in this without doubt or alarm.
Rejoice in its life-affirming presence;
Dejection and death mark its absence.

I blissfully bow to the 'Here and Now.'

Morning Beauty

The morning is slowly lifting her veil,
Revealing the beauty of hill and dale
Like a lovely bride opening her eyes
After a night of blissful sleep and sighs.

The morning air whispers in the glade,
Caressing each branch, leaf, and blade
Like a lass combing her silken tresses
Before she tries on her pretty dresses.

The dewdrops adorn blades of grass,
Quietly reflecting the color of brass,
Like tears of joy shining on the face
Of a ravished maiden in purple lace.

An amber glow of soft light has spread
Over the valley and lit its church spires,
Like a smile on the face of a well-bred
Dame – of firm faith that never expires.

The morning sun has raised its full orb
Over the valley dressed in emerald garb,
Like a celestial beauty lifting her head
Of golden locks from her heavenly bed.

The groves of trees and the rich verdure
Are inhaling the light to grow and mature
And flower like a budding young woman,
Consuming love to make another human.

The streams of the valley are awashed
In gold, melting the sunrays unabashed,
Like dancing damsels fluidly revealing
Their sinuous bodies to ignite a feeling.

The morning has stirred life in the valley.
Its domains and denizen prepare to dally,
Hugging cups of sweet tea or black coffee,
Starting their projects – whatever they be:

A parent is readying a child to go to school.
Some folks are avidly planning ways to pool
Their energy and resources for good use,
Like a resolute lady ready to ignite a fuse.

The men and women and children – all
Love their valley for it is like a cute doll
That gives them a great deal of real pride,
Like a young woman bedecked as a bride.

This blessed valley of exquisite mornings
Is a piece of paradise where no warnings
Or whistles are sounded under the sun
When a lovely lady plays nakedly in fun.

Sun and Rain

Dance of light,
Music of rain,
Nourish our life
Over and over again,
Alike in pleasure and in pain.

The rhythms
Of birth and death
That come and go
Too fast or too slow
Carry us on in a single breath.

When the sun shines,
Hearts feel warm and gay;
Sparked by the golden eye
In the bright blue sky,
We say, "What a beautiful day!"

When it rains,
We're softly wrapped
In the rich aroma of the earth,
Dripping verdure and mirth,
And by this sweet symphony enrapt.

12
Kindred Spirits

"I don't know," she asked him gravely,
"Why those birds are flying so low?
There must be a cornfield nearby,
Where the grain has shattered off

The ripened cobs; otherwise, why?"
The wind last night was mighty high;
It rattled doors and broke a window.
And she had heard a bird's high-pitched cry.

She said, "I saw shards of glass scattered
Across the room, but none in the crib,
Where our babe slept quietly all night.

"When I went up to see him this morn,
He was fast asleep – apple of my eye;
His hair was windblown and straw dry."

Then, with eyes averted, she quickly added,
"As I kissed his head, he let out a shrill cry –
Like them birds, he seemed ready to fly!"

Amazed, he asked her in a hushed voice,
"Is our little one – then one of them?"
"No," she said, "but then I don't know
Why some believe in being born twice!"

He cried, "Oh no, not that gibberish again.
I know some folks call it reincarnation!"
But he didn't know or cared to know:

The birds, with their swift wing and eye
Can see, smell, and dive from quite high.
They seek their food and rest and kin
Whenever and wherever they can find.
Their spirit isn't found in only one kind.

After a thoughtful pause, she ventured again,
"Some say consciousness connects us to all
But Avidya[1] and Maya[2] muffle its call
And, thus, our view of life remains small."

He was pzzled by her new-found views.

1 lack of knowledge, or false knowledge
2 Power by which the material world is manifested but its reality hidden behind a veil

16

Swallows

Five generations of barn swallows
Have claimed residency of a nest
Their two sleek ancestors chose
To build in my porch, facing west.

I saw the original pair first appear
In late March, surveying my place,
Checking the porch with extra care;
Then, eyeing a spot, they quickly built
A nest there, shaped like a low vase,
Nestled in a corner — with a slight tilt.

The nest's outer side was deftly girt
With small lumps of hardened dirt;
Its inside was feathered for comfort
And to protect their unborn from hurt.
I rarely saw these nesting swallows
During the day, but only once in a while,
When they darted swift as shadows,
Pursuing each other in a unique style.

The pair spent the nights together,
With their wings around each other,
The male sitting closer to the edge,
Making to his mate an avian pledge:
To raise a family from speckled eggs,
Feed them with insects caught in midair,
To strengthen their tiny wings and legs
And see them flying free here and there.

The mama bird would nod her head
Then bury her beak in his warm chest.
This game kept on going until it led
The mama to lay three eggs in the nest.

Soon the eggs hatched into tiny chicks,
Whose pale gullets I could easily see
As their yellow beaks did funny tricks
Whenever fed by their parents dotingly.

The awkward, scrawny, bald chicks
Were soon decked with slick feathers,
Alike in their parents' hues and optics.
Now, since the nest had no tethers,
They ventured out to test their wings
And see the awesome world around –
The thrills and challenges of all things
Up in the air and down on the ground.

My lovely guests left me in late May,
All the five of them, to my dismay.
I didn't realize that I had liked them so,
That their absence would make me low.
The nest was empty, as was my heart,
But, little by little, it ceased to smart.
Then, the following year, a new pair
Of swallows I saw in my porch reappear!

They were like the ones I had seen before.
And as soon as they noticed the nest,
(I couldn't their excited chirpings ignore),
They hugged it with their wings and chest.
Thereon, the new pair took its occupancy
Without any argument or further ado,
Respecting, I suppose, their urgency
Of the genetic dictate running through.

They repeated the same song and dance
As their parents had me learn before.
They too were blessed by life's chance
To raise a brood of their own to adore,
Without any visible bondage or remorse,
And then set them free on their course.

This drama played for three years more,
As three more generations of swallows
Came looking for their place of amore.
No wonder it is whence all life flows.

Scene I

When the cold north wind blows
Over the Dakota Territory,
The life on the prairie
Rises to greet the Winter Fairy.
For her arrival, it's best to remember,
She may show up as early as September.
That is why Powwows and Octoberfest
Are held around this time with native zest.

When her herald spins on his gusty nave,
The grasses roll in a shimmering wave.
The leaves hanging still on the trees,
Shake and rustle in musical keys
Before they fall to their knees
On earth's bosom to sleep.
Now is the time to apply caulk
On doors and windows to cold air block.

Scene II

Then on a gray November day,
The fairy sends us another herald,
A whirling flurry in a fleeting storm
Knocking softly on the window panes,
Showing us her smiling face — to inform
That the Winter Fairy is now on her way,
Planning for the next six months to stay
With us, making the prairie crystal gay.

As the Winter Fairy covers the prairie
In December, January, or February
With a thick mantle of dry snow,
The temperature falls low
Reaching zero
And below
Zero
And
Then
The blizzards blow.

Scene III

The Winter Fairy's noisy heralds cause no fear.
People go in and out of their homes
Bundled up in layers of looms,
Warm wool, and footware,
Topped with insulated coats 'n' caps,
While the merry flurry dances and taps,
Whitening the roofs and less traversed lanes
Of the highways that disappear on the planes.
The powdery flakes that fall freely from the sky
Cover every exposed surface that meets the eye.

The soft snow then hardens into ice — just in trice
Trees and electric wires sparkle with hanging ice.
When the holy month of December draws near,
The Dakotans like to throw parties with fanfare.
They throng the indoor malls and warm shops
To buy gifts for the families — until time stops
The search — only to resume it the next day,
If the weather cooperates the same way.
For who knows what the Winter Fairy may bring
During the night as she and her heralds dance in a ring.

❦ 15 ❦
Wind Storm

The fierce wind that blew yesterday,
Breaking trees and shattering leaves,
Flattening ripening corn in the fields,
Raising dark clouds of dust and debris,
Sweeping clean the last paved street
In the village ravaged by savage heat
Left us wondering — what could it be!

Each group translated it differently
In their own language — effectively!

The believers said it was God's wrath
Lashing us for the sins we've committed.
The scientists blamed the CO_2 emitted
By our every fossil fuel-burning activity.
Some were opposed to the latter view,
Saying climate has a cyclical proclivity,
So humans must in no way feel guilty.

I was confused by these familiar views,
So I looked for other telltale clues.

The wind had blown away my senses,
Cooled down my blood and passion,
Dried up the puddles of my pure reason,
Released me from my raw emotion.
I found myself in a different season,
Washed and wiped clean, and cheery.

Then I realized the wind had no aim,
But to lift us from being too weary
Of the monotony of a torrid season.

On Freedom

Oh freedom! you know well your noble reach,
The extent of your domain over human speech,
The limits placed on daily action and expression
That cleverly bind you with undue suppression.

You are the firmament on which men and nations
Build their hopes for a just and prosperous world,
Seeking in you the protection of their passions:
Knowledge, action, beauty, and justice – unfurled.

You make an ordinary pen mightier than a sword.
You banish oppression and lift humanity upward.
You cast out prejudice of religion, gender, and race.
You are the formidable force we lovingly embrace.

Yet you face menacing challenges from all sides:
Warring nations, disputing factions, and the like
Invoke your name in vain, taking delirious rides
In the deserts of self-serving logic – used as a dyke.

There are the fanatic Freedom Fighters who prefer
To kill their own female kin for exposing their face,
Or for claiming their right to education; so suffering
In silence the malpractices of their religion and race.

Then there are those who want cleverly to legislate
New laws of religious freedom, which could be used
As a tool against same-sex marriage, and annihilate
The freedom of sexual expression – rightfully fused.

Oh freedom, some praise you for governance alone,
And some seek you for free-market system's hunger,
Yet there are many other powers you could us loan,
Such as freedom from ignorance, pride, and anger.

Thanks-Giving

We offer our thanks once a year —
That being the Thanksgiving Day!
The rest of the days we just stare,
Not even wondering what to say.

On this day we come prepared:
Alive, grinning, and too hungry
For the Thanksgiving Day Bird
Still roasting, not getting angry.

We honor this day by devouring
Basted turkey with family mixing
And the pilgrim ghosts hovering
Over the traditional dishes fixing.

It is a day when the adult children
Come for dinner, now once a year,
To see their old folks in confusion,
Serving them still who hardly care.

We first untie the legs of the bird,
Then pull its plucked wings apart
To reach the juicy breast, preferred
By most, carved with culinary art.

Some like the drumsticks or thighs,
But all go for the cranberry sauce
And other fixings with little cries
Of joy, as their hands reach across.

When the day's delight is over,
We may silently thank our stars
For keeping the tradition, for sure,
And the guests leaving in their cars.

American Dream Life

We prefer order over chaos and believe
There's some meaning and purpose to life,
Which must be met one way or another;
So we get up in the morning, go to work
Or school, or laze around like the retired,
Who don't have to be on a set schedule.

The kitchen is the place where we love to feast
And imbibe, keeping nourished and going,
Chewing domestic issues and fresh news
Of our friends and neighbors – the world,
The warring factions in Washington, DC,
The bloody old disputes in the Middle East.

Then we pass our time shooting the breeze
With friends in our living rooms – to please
Our estranged spouses—suspended in time,
Taking our minds off the domestic discords.
Or we sportingly push our pouty girlfriends
To admire new faces, fashions, and trends.

Then there are the bedrooms we sleep in,
Alone or with another, perhaps a spouse
Or someone special – closer to our liking,
Wanting to be bound or unbound, figuring
And feigning what really counts in the bed
For winning or losing a battle in our head!

Busy or appearing to be busy in the office,
We play the game of survival with finesse
(Like children at school, cheating on tests).
Cussing, we push for political correctness.
With forked tongues we praise – to enthrall
And so deceive clients and customers and all.

Thus we impart some semblance of meaning
To our dross life of the American dreaming:
Sharpening our skills, most avidly advancing
Our information technology to divinely soar
Into a cloud of bells and whistles we so adore
To install in our lives for commerce's sake
And keep the social media constantly awake
To tune in all subjects, except the self we own.

Children are busy with video war games – still,
Some unhappy ones devise ways to mass kill.
With our eyes focused on smart handy phones,
We absently walk and drive and talk all the more,
Praising electronic gadgets, including the drones,
To impress others – especially the Crescent choir,
For it helps prevent the thinking that we really require;
But leave it for the Silicon Valley guys to acquire.

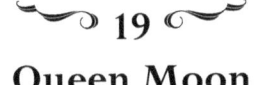

Queen Moon

"The stars around the lovely moon
Fade back and vanish very soon,
When, round and full, her silver face
Swims into sight, and lights all space."
-Sappho

The new moon is cradling the old in her arching arms,
Lending her an ebony glow from her crescent charms.
The young and old are in tight embrace as yin and yang.
The stars in the sky are still pouring out of the big bang.

I suppose numerous moons dance in our solar galaxy,
Each circling eagerly its own parent planet in ecstasy.
But is there any one comparable to our Queen Moon,
Whose stately climb in the starry sky makes us swoon?

On clear nights, your cool radiance bathes us completely.
Night by night you grow your arc to a full circle, amazingly
Soothing our hearts' longings with your cool silvery light.
O Queen Moon, you rule us benignly to our sheer delight.
When you glide over the clouds that love to kiss your feet,

You treat us to a game of hide 'n' seek as the clouds meet
And disperse to veil or unveil your face, letting your light
Lend a silver lining, turning darkness into a hopeful night.

Man and beast and trees and mighty seas are in your hold.
You make man and wild beasts sing to you in ways untold.
You let Raath-ki-Rani[1] lend its fragrance to the new bride.
You command oceans and seas to swell and roll in pride.

It is said you were once a part of earth's mantle and core,
Then a demon carried you away, which left the earth sore.
Whatever the truth, we're still intimate and love you more;
That is why we keep on sending our ships to your shore.

1 A sweet-scented flowering tree

To Sorrow

Why, O sorrow, do you sit in the kernel of my mind,
eating it away,
Layer by layer, like a treacherous worm, too unkind
in your sway?

Just for your own survival and indifferent to mine,
much too close
For comfort, pretending to be a friend – supine
in a mocking repose.

You of myriad forms and deceits are, at best, cold,
cunning, and meek.
You seek a warm, sheltering place in hearts bold,
then make them weak.

Shallow and shameless, you relentlessly prey
on sensitive souls;
Hunt and hound them until their hair turns gray with
your scolds.

Haven't I carried you tenderly as a mother would her
ailing child,
Sheltered you in my heart's ache as long as I could,
running wild.

O Sorrow, don't you know why your obligation lies
with me?
I have given you a place in my heart that cries:
I am your home and you have the key.

Insensitivity

I

It is amazing!
How can it be?
That we are okay
In our tragic loss,
Feel no despair,
Or even see
That we are still
There on the cross.

II

Our senses for sensing
Were gifted by God
Before Adam's fall,
So why is our heart
Insensitive and hard
And our sharp mind
Not so keen to hear
Their urgent call?

III

Now our feelings
For us and others
Occupy a hard,
Icy, cold center
Of indifference
That none bothers
To melt or thaw,
Lest a care may enter.

IV

Alas! we have sunk
  Deep into the earth,
  To crawl there with
  Slimy, blind worms,
  And just like them,
  Feeling no mirth,
  Nor sensing sorrow,
    We inanely spend our terms.

V

Insensitivity and indifference
  Have led us to shut
  Windows of our soul,
  Or, for some dole,
  To bargain with the devil
  In a Faustian fashion.
  We have sadly chosen
    To fall in a deep hole.

VI

O sweet oblivion!
  Go, drape us on
  With your thick
  Insensitive skin.
  Keep us etherized
  Until we are gone
  And are no more
    To rapture a kin.

Orphaned Child

I saw her once – in a trance,
A sweet little girl – about ten,
Dancing bare feet in a cobbled street
Of a heavily shelled town in France.

The sun was high in the sky,
Pouring hot and heavy
Scorching rays on every stone and soul
Underfoot and nearby.

A throng of people – young and old,
In a circle – shuffling their feet,
Watched her perform in the dizzying heat,
A wild dance – for a sou or two sold.

The child kept hopping briskly on the street
To escape the beating heat,
Shaking her hands and hips in the thin air,
Just to disclaim her fear.

She turned and twisted – bent to please,
With starved guts in rhythmic tease.
The merciless sun paused in the sky blue
And dyed her hair an amber hue.

The dance took its own time and toll.
Some were moved to toss in a sou.
As the child picked the coins for her bread,
I saw the cobblestones smeared blood-red.

A Live Shadow

The sun peeled a shadow off her face
And stamped it on a white marble wall
For the world, its eloquent lines to trace
And find how history makes us recall
The reasons for our downfall.

In profile, the face was very refined,
With an uplifted brow – broadly wise,
The nose, lips, and chin well defined,
And a swan-neck pleasing to the eyes –
Lending the shadow no disguise.

The passersby who looked at the wall
And thereon saw etched a phantom face,
Wondered whose visage it was after all.
Was its live source nearby in place
Or floating somewhere in the space?

As the sun in the west was setting low,
A strange glow lighted up the shadow,
As if it were miraculously coming to life
And about to speak of her endured strife
In a time and place with mischief rife.

Murder of innocence, and of thought,
Followed by attempts at ethnic cleansing
Of those who were selectively caught,
Because their beliefs did not coincide
With those who had power to decide.

Slowly, the live shadow faced the crowd
And began to speak – like on the celluloid:
"My country was secular – and of it proud,
Where religious differences didn't colloid,
Nor were inter-alliances disallowed.

"But soon a wind of ethnic hatred blew,
That tore the old fabric of unity asunder;
Religious zealots guns and sabers drew
To kill their "enemies" or put them under,
Actually — for easy rape and plunder.

"Families and friends were split apart,
Age-old amity wrenched from their heart.
The women had to offer their naked bodies
To fill their swollen bellies or find ways
To reach other shores without delays.

"I was one of those who met this fate —
Separated from my mom, dad, and mate,
Found refuge in a cool, sheltering country,
Where I am accepted by all and sundry
And stand rooted as a sturdy oak tree."

Having said this, the picture faded away,
Leaving us deeply affected and thinking
About the wages of intolerance we pay
And the punishment we keep on taking,
For human destiny is of our own making.

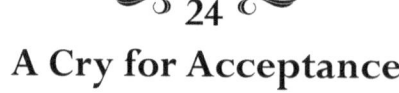

A Cry for Acceptance

Written after hearing a speech by Karen Van Fossan on
discrimination against sexual orientation, given at the
Unitarian Church in Bismarck, North Dakota

The tremulous pause before you spoke of raw injustice,
The silent prayer you made to gather poise and finesse,
The unshed tear shining in your eye as a diamond point,
Awakened the assembled few to recognize and anoint
The victims of hate and hubris conjoint.

As you made the case against prejudice and naked terror
Unleashed on those innocent of any self-conceived error,
Tormented by slurs, slashed by daggers, dragged in mud,
Sharp anguish ripped through the crowd; tears were shed
To wash the lingering stains of blood.

The men or women who find comfort in their own kind
And like to love and live together in a union so maligned
By the self-righteous primitive hoards pose no real threat
To the society or state, or ever make our good God shut
The doors of mercy on those who are differently cut.

Natural variance and struggle for survival raise this voice:
Claims of superiority in color, form, function, or choice
Rest, verily, on hollow rocks of conceit and blind belief.
Only you can bring some hope, reason, and needed relief
To those who watch in disbelief.

Mourning

It kept on coming from that open window!
On the third floor of the apartment complex
Facing mine, across the derelict lane:
A groaning sound – like persistent moaning–
Each spell extending in a droning noise,
Seemingly, from a sick old woman in pain.

I wondered if she was attended to or all alone.
This cry of anguish drove me insane.
I shut my window to muffle the sound,
But it buzzed in my head 'round and 'round.

And I couldn't take it anymore.
So I walked out of my apartment door,
Bent on doing something in this regard:
I knew not what, but it hit me hard
To be reminded how miserable life can be
As we get old and find ourselves so lonely.

Getting old is on everybody's plate,
But loneliness is a curse of fate;
It devours your life faster than you can see
A fish gobbling your proffered bait.

This teeming world is a very lonely place
To many men and women who can't face
Differences in opinion, religion, or race,
Or different expressions of sex or age.
Yet we can't keep on ignoring forever
Our common needs that bind us together.

So I sped quickly to the other building
And met the apartment manager in his office.

He said, "Yes, an old woman lived in that unit,
Alone with her golden retriever – crazy a bit.
But she died yesterday, and since then her dog
Has been mourning – piteously groaning."

The Fruit of Sin

The air in the Great Hall was heavy with grief.
It crawled on the floor in eerie swirls.
It clung to the columns in creepy curls.
All assembled there were staring in disbelief.

Sitting motionless on the hardwood chairs
Around a coffin, wherein lay the cold
Body of a woman — twenty years old,
The mourners were holding back their tears.

She had died in sleep of an unknown cause.
The few who seemingly knew her well
Couldn't, for shock or fear, see or tell
What the cause of her untimely death was.

None of them but one knew for sure
Whence and why she had come there,
But they weren't dumb or lacking care
Not to sense she was stricken and poor.

Miss Lisa had come from a big metropolis.
She was a front teller in a high-rise bank,
Good at numbers, also fearless and frank,
With no idea she would end up in a necropolis.

She had come in search of a former lover,
Who had embezzled from his workplace
And was now in this town, hiding his face
After making her pregnant in his bower.

The wicked lover saw Lisa in his pursuit,
Trailing him to this out-of-the-way town.
Sensing arrest, he so feared for his crown
And planned to snuff her out — like a brute.

One night he went to her rented quarter,
Begging her forgiveness on his two knees,
Gaining her trust with his faked apologies.
But the wretch was planning her murder.

After making up with a few nice words said,
Poor Lisa fell asleep on the rumpled bed.
He placed a pillow on her upturned head
And with demonic force choked her dead.

He wasn't troubled by this dastardly act,
But emboldened to play it out to the hilt.
To divert public attention from his guilt,
He anonymously called the police to react.

The authorities found Lisa dead in her room,
With no definite clues that would lead
To the person who committed this deed —
Save a coat button in the bristles of a broom.

Lisa's body was placed in the Hall for a reason:
To see if her wily killer was still around,
And if lured, he could be so easily bound;
For a criminal betrays himself in due season.

So Lisa's killer too went to the Great Hall,
Pretending cleverly to be a deeply caring soul,
Hiding his identity like an embedded mole,
But he couldn't keep up this masquerade at all.

For a button was missing on the culprit's coat.
The rest were similar to one they had found
At the scene of crime; so he was duly bound
For questioning and found guilty by the court.

This story was related to me by a friend of mine
Who was a fine police detective in his time
And by effort and luck solved many a crime.
He concluded: "Adam's progeny is not that fine."

Adding, "We are the inheritors of a hungry knife,
Wielded first by Abraham on his own son
To gain favor in the eyes of the Great One;
This curse assumes many forms in our selfish life."

I told my friend, "This analogy doesn't fit the story."
He answered, "Love's fruit isn't always sweet,
Like the apple of Eden's tree, we mustn't eat,
And if we do, we do surely provoke God's furry."

Affliction

I opened my eyes after a blissful night,
But she had left, taking her bags along.
Only her perfume was lingering on
In the bedroom, where I didn't belong.

I thought she had gone to get some air
Or drink something to wake her up
And be ready to show again her flair
After she had emptied one more teacup.

But when she didn't show up by noon,
I began to wonder: what could it be
That tore her away from me so soon,
When she had all night clung to me?

A searing pain shot through my heart.
Weird phantoms sat on my chest
And kept pounding me a whole lot,
Asking questions I couldn't answer best.

When I was beat and at my wits' end,
The telephone rang and broke my spell.
It was she, telling me, "I had to attend
An early Mass for a guilt feeling to quell."

See, we had met only a month before
At a resort and sown mutual affection;
I was a drifter, ready to come ashore,
But she was fighting a moral affliction.

Contradiction

She is against all
Forms of tyranny,
Including irony,
Except her own,
To which she ascribes,
By extension and *a-priori*,
A noble intention *post-priori*.

If asked to answer
An innocent question,
It is naked aggression
That must be quickly nipped,
Lest it becomes a contention
So unworthy, so unbecoming,
Of her attention – sitting or standing.

She is against
Bias and prejudice
For race, sex, age, or disability,
Practiced or weakly regulated;
But her heart is bent on rewarding
Those who have no cause or standing
If she finds they are in her political kettle,
Or if her eyes on them amorously settle.

Indifference

There is a framed picture of my mom and dad
On my bedroom wall, facing east.
It catches the morning sun and the moonlight,
But not to my complete delight.

I don't look at the picture as often as I should,
Not because it is on my back,
But the light cast off the glass blinds my view
Of the persons in the picture true.

I have ignored too long to do what would be right:
Move the picture to a better site
So I might lay my eyes on the oft-forgotten faces,
Who beckon me to recall my traces —

Traces of the bygone childhood days happily spent
On or close to my mother's lap,
Gazing at her face, listening to her sweet lullaby,
With my father fussing nearby.

Also, of the days when school and games held sway,
And away from home I went
Their eyes following, filled with hope and pride,
Or anguished when defeated I cried.

Their gentle guidance throughout my early life —
The steady beacon that lighted
Each bend and curve of the life's highway —
I took Moving forward, without a backward look!

My all too craving self assumed a robotic routine,
Held me captive to trite demands of life
And made me woefully forget my real aim:
To know myself, I must know whence I came.

Work for livelihood kept me busy during the day;
Familial chores took evenings and nights away.
Thus the faces of my dear parents framed in my heart,
As in the picture on the wall, faded a lot.

Dear God, my sin of indifference has cost me dearly.
I am abysmally ashamed to have acted so poorly.
In disowning my source, I have disowned myself;
Oh mercy! how can I bridge this enormous gulf?

Equus, My Equus

Equus! Equus! show me the way.
Don't hesitate, tremble, or sway,
For a noble path we must take;
Truth and beauty as one, we must make.
Our new destiny we must boldly face.
In this quest, doubt or fear has no place.

Equus, dear, you are strong and fair,
Of noble birth from a proud sire
And a beautiful mare, both full of fire.
So I don't see how can we tire
On this journey that we undertake,
For we have our decisions to make.

You remember my grand old man —
A dashing doctor of great repute,
Who could help a mare bear her foal
And bring it out intact, body and soul!
Your ma and pa were mighty proud
When they saw you, neighing aloud.

You were born a feisty chestnut brown,
With a white star on your noble crown.
You've white socks on all of your feet.
Your mane lashes the wind as you fleet.
I comb your long lustrous tail every day,
Brush your flanks as you nibble your hay.

You love apples and sugarcoated oats
And dream of jumping over the moats
To castles where captive maidens languish
And expect me to free them from anguish.
Equus, the old ways of conquest are gone.
Now we've to cross a different Rubicon.

You and I have traversed arduous roads,
But none as difficult as the one that bodes
Death of character through lack of courage
And loss of faith in the truth-in-beauty adage.
Equus, didn't I ask you to show me the way?
So give me strength to carry my cross, I say.

Dear Partner

Fifty hot summers and fifty cold winters
You and I have deftly weathered together,
And between the two, in spring and fall,
Planted roses for attar[1] and colors to gather.

In our own small way, we made it through
The forest of life; even as the mists appeared
To block or let the sunlight come through,
We kept on driving forward so undeterred.

Each of us brought our strengths to bear
On the demands of relationship and care,
Facing toughest challenges without fear
The simple labors that too wear and tear.

Our passions weren't of a particular kind:
Love of reading and gardening we shared;
In cooking and cleaning we always shined,
But in the choice of music a little differed.

Our love for each other had its own phases,
Like the monthly cycle of moon in the sky –
Waxing and waning, feigning to ignore
Our cravings, but never failing to gratify.

In the early and mid sections of our life,
We would chase each other with desire –
Deeply intense and persistent in its demand,
And every time each other's faculty admire.

And we were duly blessed with children,
Whose achievements made us very proud,
For services they rendered to their country,
Which made them stand out in a big crowd.

---

1 Essence of roses

Today, at seventy-four, you are the same
Woman who I have loved in my own way.
But I wouldn't dare call you my old flame,
For you'll quit speaking on your birthday —
Which is today! And I say, "Happy birthday."

Daughter

Like earth, the bringer of life and bounty,
Like air, the ensurer of breath and beauty,
Like water, the awakener of spirit and body,
Like fire, power supreme and purifier of all,
Daughter, you are the life-giving mother
Of mankind, blessed and kind,
A treasure to find.

In you, daughter, resides the strength
Of fire and the music of water in motion,
The healing touch of air present all around,
The blue glow of the earth seen from afar.
Daughter, you bring purpose to mankind,
Joy to man, solace to child,
Soothingly styled.

Your name has a deep meaning, Seema.
It was given to you by your doting mama,
Defining the expanding frontier or territory
Of an empire, or any thought's trajectory
Acquired by the sheer brilliance of mind
And endeavor of the right kind
That the wise find.

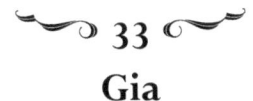

Gia

When I heard the first cry of life
Issue from your trembling lips,
Taking in the first divine breath,
I felt a tingling in my fingertips.

A chorus of joyous feelings arose
In symphony, like strings of light,
When we caught the awesome sight
Of a child, lovely as a perfect rose.

Suffused by your mother's love,
You came regally to rule and tame
Our hearts and minds in your name,
Gabrielle S.T., our cute little dove.

They groomed you at a petite sink;
The nurse's hands were full and pink.
Papa stood nearby to see and show.
You held his pinky and didn't let go.

Neatly swaddled, you went to see
Your dear mama and whispered
Quietly in her ear, "It is me, Gia.
Come to show the way forward."

Your mama kissed your crown
And, pulling you close to her heart,
Whispered, "Yes, love, why not?
Say, are your eyes blue or brown?"

Then you looked deep into her eyes
And whispered this: "Does it matter:
Hue, color, or love? I take the latter;
For that is the truth that never lies."

To My Children

There are joys — but none so great
As living your life in a peaceful state,
Without strife, sorrow, or merciless fate,
And drinking from life at a steady rate.

The aims of life shift as grains of sand.
They seem real until we truly understand
The color and contour of the very land,
The mountain or valley where we stand.

Our senses and soul must clearly behold
The merits in ideas on which we are sold,
The acts we commit that seem so bold;
Thus we see what is and isn't real gold.

None of this is totally unknown to you,
For you have stood in that awesome pew
Of the morphing world, where just a few
Become self-aware and are reborn anew.

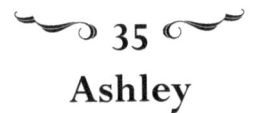

Ashley

Oh Ashley, sweet, bright, lovely child, light of my eye:
How deeply happy and blessed we are. Don't ask why;
As you grow, you will know how stars shine in the sky,
How little buds drink the rainbow and bloom by and by.

Oh Ashley, sweet, bright, lovely child, light of my eye:
You came in a storm, your will and strength made it shy.
It hovered briefly and then vanished with a wimpy cry.
You won fair and square; we thanked God, the most high.

Oh Ashley, sweet, bright, lovely child, light of my eye:
As your mom-dad-bro were trying to know you better,
My Rose of Austin would roll her eyes in anger and cry,
"Where is Papa? It ain't fair; I want him here and nearby."

Oh Ashley, sweet, bright, lovely child, look into my eye:
For four weeks your papa turned and tossed.
Ask why. Just to hold my dear granddaughter, my little cutie pie,
Touch her dainty hands and feet, and sing her a lullaby:
"Sweet wonder and delight, oh precious light of my eye."

To Stephen D. Merrill

"Sweet are the pleasures that to verse belong,
And doubly sweet a brotherhood in song."
-John Keats

My dear friend, Doc Stephen,
I'm blessed in your friendship,
Which began a long time ago
In a college town in Colorado,
Where our views found a kinship.

We were there for a meeting
Focused on land and crop sciences,
Going over new ideas and advances,
But, learning more while eating
At the funky 'Bottoms Up' Diner,
Where the fare was quite delicious
And our conversation sumptuous.
Nothing else could have been finer.

Moving from subject to subject,
We chewed on some philosophies,
Social and political controversies,
Without a specific aim or object.
Thus discovering mutual interests,
We developed a lasting friendship
That neither imposed any hardship
Nor turned us into crazy sophists.

Then, in North Dakota, life was easy:
You working for the Big Brother
And I for another, —a lot smaller —
But both in Land Reclamation busy.
Your wedge plots at Center and Stanton
Yielded information that helped change
The state's reclamation rules — to manage
The replacement of soil on the overburden.

Your interest in saving the environment
From misuse — out of greed we betray —
Still continues in your own charming way
And fills me with pure amazement.
There are other passions too that stir you:
Foreign languages, cultures, and faces,
Which beckon you to far-flung places,
Since all forms of prejudice you eschew.

There came to us a time of adventure
When we traveled through teeming India,
The land of Rama, Krishna, and Buddha,
Where diverse races and faiths anchor
Their hopes in freedom and democracy,
Based on the principles of Dharma yoga
And a firm belief in the power of karma,
That led to their intellectual aristocracy.

Remember the places and people we saw,
The research and admin centers, as they go,
The lust for life carved in stones at Khajuraho,
The turbaned tribals pulling on a hookah,
My nephew's wedding with a cute doctor
Clad in fine silks, smiles, and laughter,
Our reception and presentations at the HAU,
And the majestic Taj Mahal's incredible view.

As the years have bleached our heads,
The brotherly affection we have shown
Has spread its strong roots and grown,
Connecting our lives and family threads.
But there is so much more to this story:
For there are so many virtues I have seen
In you, Steve, which a world to me mean.
Had I some, it would add to our glory.

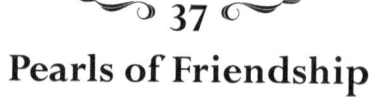

Pearls of Friendship

When you laid your pearls in front of my eyes,
String by string, with a soft glow and a smile,
Each unique, yet each with pearls of the same size,
I heard you both, as it were, from a distant isle,
Talking as Neptune's daughters, to my surprise,
Of ideas in verses that render substance to style.

The pearls spoke mutely of their radiant beauty,
Granted them by the deep ocean and the clam.
You radiated your impeccable self with plenty
Of poise, coming from an awareness of "I Am"
That brings one closer to truth and humanity,
Like rain, rivulets, and streams rush to fill a dam.

The luster of some personalities can't be hid,
Be it a cloudy, rainy, or dreary day at work.
Standing by a counter or hidden under a lid,
Neither you nor the pearls can one dare shirk,
For that would demean elegance, God forbid,
And make the good-intentioned person a jerk.

Your emphatic call to form a vernal fellowship
Is a soothing idea and accepted with gratitude;
For there may grow a shiny pearl of friendship,
Just as a fading rose – growing in its certitude
Of life's brevity – sees beauty in a bee's kinship
And thus frees itself of the thorns of solitude.

Reminiscent

She is an auditory expert,
Well versed in sensory art,
But when I saw her first,
From both near and afar,
She faintly reminded me of
An exceptional work of art.

She seemed to have alighted
Softly from a museum wall
And is now working in a hall
Where patients are delighted
To see that their dim hearing
Can be cured easily, after all.
In a white lab coat walks she,
But I wonder who it could be.

She has an enigmatic smile
And a dreamy, distant gaze
(That artists like to capture)
And throws you into a maze
Of high-tech auditory-exam
In her clinic's cloistered isle.
She keeps the record on file
To get a picture of the sensory style.

Now it suddenly comes to me
That in her face and art
Is a semblance of a sort
Of a Florentine thought:
In Nicole, Mona Lisa you see,
In her scientific art, da Vince.

Out of Memory

We were sitting outside on the porch,
Sipping cold coffee – with averted eyes,
Fearing conversation may snap our ties,
And the sharp sunlight may hit our eyes.

But I couldn't help asking the question:
"Did we ever have any joy in our lives?"
At this, she rose and silently sped away,
Leaving me there with a sense of dismay.

I turned my head toward the dry yard –
Baked hard by the sun, thirsting for rain.
The few plants standing still were in pain;
At this desolation, my hope was charred.

She walked back to the porch and said,
"How come you don't irrigate the lawn?"
I remained quiet, uncertainly withdrawn,
And led my tired legs toward the shed.

There I sank in a chair to take a break.
My long life flashed by me stage by stage;
The childhood, youth, prime, and old age,
Had been spent in trying my life to make.

But now I couldn't my priorities rethink,
Or figure out easily which turn to take;
Too much was on my plate and at stake.
Whatever I did would raise another stink.

She knew our water supply had been cut
For not having paid our bills on time.
But she couldn't this ladder easily climb,
For she had her mind from all reality shut.

I had seen this symptom in some old-timers
But never thought her condition to be serious,
Until her spells became frequent and obvious.
Then my love was found to have Alzheimer's.

Silent Treatment

Don't mock me with your silence.
It harms me not, but only you.
Your consuming pride and ego
Are at work — hardly affecting me.

Silent treatments won't make me cry,
But they make you fall from my eye.
You have played this game before
Without eliciting from me any reply.

Your vanity has inflated your ego,
Covering you in its dark veil,
Making you walk like a shadow,
Silently screaming, "Hell," to no avail.

Beauty is a noble gift; wear it well.
Pleasant speech adds to its content,
For it is the expression that can tell
If you are a beauty or a malcontent.

Silence has many hues and meanings.
When used wisely, it is golden.
When used in rancor, it is rotten.
Reach inside to figure your feelings.

There is a centering light in all of us.
It is the source and seat of conscience,
Always there to provide us guidance.
Just look for it with some eagerness.

Mirage

When shallow waters are deemed too darn deep,
And the nanny goats are mistaken for woolly sheep,
The watchdogs are taking a deep, oblivious sleep.

When mere shadows are seen as solid substance,
And important decisions are made in an instance,
The watchdogs are looking from a foggy distance.

When dream castles are built out of crystal sand,
And water lilies are planted on the arid highland,
The watchdogs are dancing crazy in a merry band.

When justice is played a glossy painted lip service,
And the bureaucratic tape binds each in its service,
The watchdogs are busy doing a great disservice.

When the selfish rich ride the horse named Charity,
And dancing showgirls reveal much in sheer clarity,
The watchdogs can't help but become openly flirty.

When a lusty jackass can't get a good night's rest
And wanders from bed to bed as a pesky love pest,
The watchdogs are also taking turns in this quest.

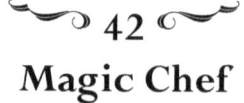

Magic Chef

You are a skilled chopper and dicer
Of onion, garlic, celery, and cicer.
You're a magic chef — a gourmet Kaiser.

You know how to neatly spice a dish,
Be it of veggies, mutton, beef, pork, or fish.
You're a magic chef — hard to vanquish.

You prefer using spices from the East:
Coriander, cumin, and ginger, at least.
You're a magic chef — a turmeric artiste.

You don't like the Italian flavors to bypass:
Basil, rosemary, oregano, and lemongrass.
You are a magic chef, admired by every lass.

You serve truth with a touch of lime.
You roast lies with a dash of thyme.
You're, indeed, a magic chef sublime.

You toss exotic condiments with finesse,
Cinnamon, cardamom, nutmeg to caress.
You're a magic chef who truly pleases us.

Elements

The snow on the deck has melted and gone.
Green grass is trying to emerge in the lawn,
Pressing its pale, tender tips against the cold,
Crusty ice pinning it with unyielding hold.

Now, let us see, whose effort wins the race,
White Goliath or David Green, as they face
Each other in a deadly mortal embrace,
Their destiny determined by nature's pace?

The tepid sun, as yet in its early March run,
Is not sure how to help the grass and be done,
For it is also wrestling to break the crusty ice
And in this struggle keeps on rolling the dice.

My love, none can avoid the struggles of life.
They give us wisdom through pain and strife.
David Green, the grass, is meek and humble,
But, in its great struggle, it does not tremble.

I have no doubt the sun will soon take away
The icy blues that have spread in the usual way
On each face and feature across the landscape
And restore our fallen spirits without escape.

Spring Eternal

The sun is slowly rising
Out of a vast live basin,
Shimmering liquid gold.

My heart is just emerging
Out of a deep, icy gloom
Into your blissful fold.

The light is now warming
The weary, cold east face
Of the mountain so old.

The spring is finally here,
With its color and music,
And I am no longer cold.

O spring! joyously fresh
Sun and rain you bring,
Rekindling hopes untold.

Now, I am also awaiting
The spring of my youth
To make me feel as bold !

Promised Summer

Oh sweet little bird, I hear
You sing of coming summer,
When the spring is still here
In winter's whimsical care.

Far in the north, do we dare
Assume that seasons are fair
And their cycles quite clear,
But for your presence, dear!

So proclaim loudly, my fair
Angel of hope, without fear,
And bring the promised air.
I too shall lay my heart bare

And sing with you with flair,
For those who feel and hear
The coming of summer near
On the wings of hope, dear.

Snow Geese

The framed shadows on my wall,
Colored in the gray demon's gall,
Raise their grim voices in a chorus,
Shouting, "Hang it, don't blame us."

I guess I am formed of dense clay;
Most things around me seem gray.
Thinking in circles devours my day;
In the valley of dark shadows I lay.

Should I stay or go away? Or think!
If I stay, I won't see that ray of light.
If I go, should I discard my baggage?
In this lies my blurred image.

Or stand on the granite seashore
And implore the mighty tides to restore
The broken wings of my thought,
So I may fly to wherever I ought:

Over the fields of ripening grain,
Over the emerald islands
About to rise again
And float there in the crisp blue air.

Or should I ask the silver moon
To relieve me of my baggage
And cast it on the tides of oblivion,
Where I can't gather it anymore.

Now, if the sea and moon see it fit
To grant me this boon,
I will become light and feel restored
To fly with the snow geese—soon.

Go South

Oh!
Let us go
To the south,
To the warm south,
Where the sun hangs low
And the ocean breeze
Blows with ease
As we go.
Oh!
Let us go
To the south,
To the balmy south,
Where red clouds break
Into rain and flow
Slowly below
To slake.
Oh!
Let us go
To the south,
To the exotic south,
Where love is in the air,
With its fragrance
Everywhere,
My dear.
Oh!
Let us go
To the south,
To the magical south,
Where a fantastic altitude
To Gabriel's Realism
Was attained in
Solitude.

Learn from Regret

I

How soon we forget
Remorse and regret!
And fall back again
In the same old rut
Of loving and hating,
Baiting and cheating.

II

Then, finding a way
To peacefully lay
With our conscience
By faking penitence,
Calling it repentance
To gain acceptance.

III

This – a sly technique
Is, indeed, so unique!
For it easily redeems
Us in our own eyes
And the clergy guys'.
Never mind who lies!

IV

Forgetting your sins
Is like storing in bins
The trash you owned,
But never ever let go.
It'll keep on growing,
As grass after mowing.

V

Remorse would help
Save us from ourselves,
Only if it stays with us
To infuse and harness
The wisdom we need
And must always heed.

VI

It will not let us repeat
The mistakes that beat
Us over and over again,
And our strength drain.
So learn from remorse,
For it is a rich resource.

VII

Then we will not regret
Once again or ever fret
In choosing our friends,
Lovers, words, or trends;
For in our past remorse,
We find the right course,

VIII

Which is smarter to take
Than tempting a snake,
Whose sexy-vexy form
Would do us great harm.
So reject but don't forget
Past remorse and regret.

Part II

Reflections on Love

Love

"Love" is the name for our
pursuit of wholeness
for our desire to be complete."
-Plato, The Symposium

"I am the poet's elation,
And the artist's revelation,
And the musician's inspiration."
-Khalil Gibran, "Song of Love"

Love's Abode

Is it in the heart
Or in the mind where
Love dwells? Or there
In the soul, as "thou art"?

Love, your forms are infinite
In your purpose, shape, and scope;
You dwell in the quark, and string
The universe in its manifest hope.

You dwell in the blades of grass,
In the shrubs and trees that pass
Your grandeur in rich showers
Of color and scent of flowers.

You are in the mother's milk,
In the morphed cocoon of silk.
You are on the lips of an infant
And in the eyes of a supplicant.

You are in the innocent smile,
As rays of light with no guile.
You shine in the morning dew,
And the tear dropped for you.

You are in the core of a stone
And on the wings of a tide and tone.
All things inanimate or animate,
Rich or poor, find you incarnate.

Incarnate in them, within and around.
You suffuse each and then surround,
Leaving no space or second untouched,
No thought or act — fetched or unfetched.

Though readily visible is your face
In the lovers' kiss and embrace,
Allow us to see clearly your real charm
In its supreme singularity and divine form.

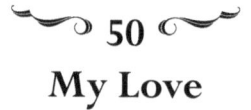

My Love

As the sun brings the day to my door
In warm waves of light and much more;
As the moon casts shadows on the floor,
Touching my mortal frame to explore;
You, my love, reach deep into my soul,
With unsaid words scoring their goal.

You speak with eyes that shine, as before,
Of love that binds soul to soul and more.
And in purest form is bound to adore
All in close kinship with God at its core.
Yes, my darling, you awakened my soul
By a look in your eyes adorned with kohl.

Your generous gift of love and friendship,
Your gorgeous charm and gentle kinship,
Your ceaseless caring and selfless sharing,
Your joys and fears quite readily nearing,
Fill your eyes with warm mist and rain,
Washing away all my life's pain and strain.

But now I'm sitting here all alone,
Thinking of how fast our time has flown.
Your each soulful gesture remains alive,
Giving me will and strength to survive.
Wherever I go, I see and carry your light —
As the sun in the day and moon in the night.

I Love You

"How do I love thee? Let me count the ways.
I love thee to the depth and breadth and height
My soul can reach, when feeling out of sight
For the ends of being and ideal Grace."
-Elizabeth Barrett Browning, "Sonnet XLIII"

I want to hold you tenderly in my gaze,
Through the spring thaws and summer blaze,
From violet dusk to golden dawn, and on and on,
Until my heart is at rest and I am gone.

Touch your face and trace your flitting shadow
In the west wind — stirring petals in the meadow
Or stand on life's shore to own one more wave —
So I too am born again with the love you gave.

Feel your sweet breath in my veins, stimulating
My senses and soul, a single cool-flame making;
Your passionate promises make me live and bold
And happily cast me in their enchanting mold.

Drink the cup of life sweetened by your song
Of love and light, with wisdom teaming along,
That you sing gracefully with heavenly charm
And draw all my senses to your earthly form.

From dust to flesh and from flesh back to dust,
Only hope remains, which too may rot or rust;
For bound we are to unending cycles of change,
But love alone saves life from being too strange.

I
Spring

Daffodils arrived in the morning,
Suddenly announcing spring;
Cool-scented air filled the valley below
The mountains, still capped with snow,
Reflecting the golden glow of the morning sun.

Your hazel eyes caught the tender
Gleam of a long-forgotten dream
And opened wide in surprise;
The daffodil stood before you as a bride,
Touching your face with love and pride.

II
Summer

In the sumptuous heat of the midday sun,
Summer arrived with a warm breeze.
Swarms of humming bees kiss flowers
Joyously, sipping nectar with artful ease.
The bees are happy, rid of winter freeze.

You're standing in a chemise over the breast.
Pearls of sweat adorn your neck and chest.
A sensuous fragrance surrounds your body.
The summer haze works in strange ways,
Reminding you of the joys of bygone days.

III
Autumn

Autumn entered at dusk with bushels of grain.
The trees are heaving under the ripening strain
Of pears, apples, and apricots — ready to be sold.
The leaves are turning purple, red, and gold.
The nights are beginning to feel pleasantly cold.

Your face is framed in curls of flaming hair,
The autumn breeze blowing it here and there.
A faint smile lights up your eyes,
Hiding a sweet secret memory behind the veil.
Yes, a tender loving time must now prevail.

IV
Winter

Lo! the night has fallen in a heap of snow;
dancing flakes are crowding the turbid sky.
Soon icy winds will blow high and low.
Crackling fires are lit in the fireplaces,
Warming the loving hearts in right places.

You are looking through a frosted pane,
Wondering when he will appear in your lane,
Hold you in a warm embrace, and kiss your face.
Lo and behold! He is at your door, ready to enter
The home of his dreams — your heart's center.

The Soul Mate

When I was in the saddle of my youth,
Surrounded by comfort and plentitude,
Cherishing books, fine foods, and friends,
Enjoying all the in-fashion trends,
Only one thing vexed my attitude:
The absence of a soulmate in my solitude.

I hadn't seen her earthly form before,
But her spirit was knocking at my door.
I searched for her in the human streams
As she kept on appearing in my dreams.
This tension stretched me day by day
As her soul in my heart dormant lay.

Then, one day, I saw her face-to-face
At a mutual friend's place.
She was standing in a corner of the room;
One look at her banished my gloom.
She introduced herself with a knowing smile;
Time sped backward on the clock's dial:

My past came back to me.
At the far end of time's tunnel stood she;
We were only specks of consciousness then,
In the universe of being and becoming, when
The souls wandered in search of each other
To fulfill God's design of bringing them together.

Beholden

To you, my love, I am most beholden,
As the rainbow is to its father golden,
As the stream to its preserving banks
And its solid bed and verdurous flanks;
  Without you, I wouldn't be.

You have brought sunshine in my life,
  Helped me cope with all my strife,
Taught me to read between the lines,
To discover the real meaning of signs;
  Without you, I wouldn't know

That there is a garden within our soul,
And its cultivation should be our goal.
If we want to see and smell the flowers,
  We must prove to be faithful lovers;
  Without you, it wouldn't be so.

For time stands still in your embrace.
Sunshine illumines a desire in your face,
Filling my heart and quickening its pace.
Uncertainty vanishes with God's grace;
  Without you, it wouldn't be true.

When we hold each other tenderly
And make our desires known honestly,
Their fulfillment presents no difficulty.
The garden in our soul has this faculty;
  With you, all my dreams come true.

Your Smile

Your smile is like the unfolding of a flower
After the morning fog and a gentle shower,
Leaving behind the sparkling diamond dew
On the petals, as on your lips painted anew.

Your smile is like a perfumed ocean breeze,
Blowing at night through the jasmine trees,
Providing relief from the wearing hot day
To those who can't sleep and restless lay.

Your smile is like a rising crescent moon
Playing with her starry friends that swoon
At her majestic glide through the night sky,
Bringing an acute desire in the lover's eye.

Your smile is like a cup of sparkling wine
That bubbles with life and invites to dine
At a well-laid table in the restaurant grand,
With music pouring from a lively band.

Your smile is like the recurring dream
That beckons me, like the lighthouse beam,
To come ashore from the sea of my despair
And hold you close, so that our hearts repair.

Dreamed Ecstasy

I am trying to recall
A half-remembered dream
But can't piece it together all,
For time is a fast-flowing stream.

We were reposing on its bank,
In the tall, clumpy, green grass,
Seasonally thick and rank,
Eyeing the bridge that reached across.

The waters crashed on the boulders,
Rousing passion in the stream;
We clasped each other's shoulders,
Thrilled by the tossed spray and steam.

It fogged the banks and our brains,
Pressing us to be nearer and nearer,
Melding into one, releasing the reins
That had kept us from being closer.

It was like a dream fulfilled,
Long abandoned to the subconscious,
Where it was held choked and stilled;
Of this pain we were fully conscious.

Lying there in the tall grass
That afternoon, with sun piercing the mist,
Casting a rainbow on my lovely lass –
I now recall: we more than simply kissed.

Your Love Dance

"O, learn to love, the lesson is but plain,
And once made perfect, never lost again."
-William Shakespeare, Venus and Adonis

You love with a heart wild with desire;
It shows in every dancing step you take. I
am carried away by your hidden fire;
It lifts me higher for your and my sake,
Allowing us both to touch the rainbow
Arching the heavens in a colorful show.
As my arms circle your waist, sparks fly.

Your lovely eyes catch the golden glare
Of Apollo, rising from his restful sleep,
Then reflect it with a jaunty flare.
This amazing spark you admirably keep,
With all the play and wisdom combined
That the gods on anyone shined.
In your eyes, many colors of love I find.

In the evenings, when the fiery hot sun
Eases into the cool bosom of the blue sea,
Painting the horizon in crimson and dun,
You let your red locks down to hold me,
By the tendrils of an amber vine treading,
My heart's chambers threading – silently;
You know the passion it kindles in me!

As the evening greets the promising night,
After a repast of delicious food and drink,
You and I curl together as we fancy right,
Without letting our lighted senses blink.
For the night is still young and yearning
To learn more from each other's turning;
I fulfill your needs, and you do mine.

Your love dance is not of the usual kind,
Neither blindly physical nor etherized,
But graced with a movement so refined
That it appears to be divinely actualized,
Lifting us both up into the ethereal skies
Where love's pure ecstasy fills our eyes,
Making us see: love-making is divine.

You love with all your body, mind, and soul,
A gift given to you by gods, as Venus was;
But you make your Adonis bold and whole,
Letting him shed his coyness for the cause.
No mortal woman has easily gained this art,
Unless she was some god's consort.
I gratefully thank the gods, for you are mine.

Passion

As you approach me in your armed splendor,
Aiming your barbed spear at my heart's chamber,
I tremble timorously in much-awaited delight;
My heart leaps forth with no trace of fright.

Love, my sweet enemy, you are ready to invade
The core of my being, yet I mustn't stop or evade
You with my hesitance, but yield my ground
Before your passion is spent and ecstasy found.

Allow me first to assemble my bearing and breath
To make your victory worth your quick death,
Which surely you shall find in my mortal embrace;
So, why not call on eternity to save your face.

But if you insist on taking me in your own way,
Be ready to see my virgin blood – that wager I lay.
Think twice before your desires overflow the dam,
For love and passion must evenly mix and flow.

I'm eager and ready to dance with you, my love,
If you only wait awhile and see how and why
It must begin and end in ecstasy, not in sorrow.
Come again in splendor and wake me tomorrow.

A Tribute to You

How can your charm ever so fade
When all this at your feet is laid:
A heart full of love and adoration,
A head bowing low in admiration?

My eyes catch a fleeting shadow:
You! amid lilies in the meadow,
Where butterflies seem confused
By the heavenly scent so diffused.

Love, time has no power over you,
For he too is so captivated by you
And slows down his steeds to see
Which celestial being it could be!

Is it Dianna, Minerva, or Olympia?
One or all! Singing in symphonia,
Playing under the pale olive trees,
Feeding sweet music to the breeze.

O! for a woman to be gods' worthy,
She must be celestial; but, if earthly,
She must surpass others in beauty,
Charm, and wit in measures plenty.

Since you are earthy, full of charm,
With lively wit and wisdom warm,
Spread your fiery wings like a lark,
And fly high to catch Apollo's spark.

Or, better, return my love as before;
I promise I'll cherish you even more
Than the gods whom you so adore —
From a long-deserted, foggy shore.

Where Your Beauty Lies

Where shall your beauty go
When you're near sixty or so?
You look still quite youthful;
I am being absolutely truthful.
Be not afraid to hear me say
What I have enjoyed each day
That tied our past to future,
As I see it happening in nature.

Your smooth and silky hair,
With which you deftly snare;
Your cool, unwrinkled brow,
Touching the clouds above;
Your shy emerald-green eyes,
Where your real power lies;
Your sweet lips painted red,
Which invite me to the bed;
Your smooth alabaster skin,
Whose luster makes heads spin;
Your bare, sloping shoulders,
Which pure admiration spur;
Your divinely shaped breasts,
Which all my attention arrest;
Your tapered waist to pelvis,
Draped in an exquisite challis —

All these marvelous attributes,
Which garner many tributes,
Will progressively fade away;
But my love will not decay,
For I wasn't merely interested
In your bodily charms listed,
But in the beauty of your mind
And soul that always shined.

Love and Freedom

As the morning freeze on the windshield
To the warming breeze does easily yield,
So shall the chill that weakens our will
Thaw when your voice the void shall fill.

The space stretched betwixt you and me
Is a fine fabric whose knots we can't see
Or untie; they're elastic bonds of love,
Which unite us and set us free somehow.

Love binds one to another, freeing each
Of isolation and despair, so we can reach
That place of freedom, which gives hope
Its wings to uplift life to its fullest scope.

Love asks none to set aside or surrender
Their identity or free will, or to render
Service burdensome to one or the other,
But fills their space with joy and wonder.

Yet there are those who define freedom
In terms of its ability to dispel boredom
By allowing them to sleep with anyone;
But is it freedom or a devouring demon?

So, my darling, thaw your frosty silence.
Let your thoughts pour out in a balance,
And define your desire with some clarity;
For freedom-giving love is not so flirty.

Pursuit

Her eyes were
Dancing,
His eyes were
Prancing,
Until their eyes
Slid into a tango,
The bongo drums
Kept on beating,
Their hearts eating
The old-love crumbs.

This game of pursuit
Is exciting, as it seems
Just like the racehorses,
Who like to run in teams
To reach their destination
Before Miss Fortune crosses.

If they see encouraging signs
And a sudden spark that shines
In the eyes of their new partners,
They sense success in these augurs
And hang their hopes on this belief,
Then keep dancing with some relief.

Hello, dear
How I fear
You there
I here

Far or near
Don't fear
You'll hear
I'll be there

If you care
Then share
Truth or dare
Be near

Yes, I care
And in fear
Drop a tear
For love is rare

Cheer Up

Cheer up, my darling sweet.
After 5pm have something to eat
And stay away from summer heat.
Also, keep away from a pesky lout
There is nothing left to beat about
In the bush, but only to retreat
To a safe corner in the street;
This I entreat.

Marquez opened our eyes
To life's surprise after surprise,
With his '*Hundred Years of Solitude*'
And '*Of Love and Other Demons,*' telling
Of omens, half-truths, and half-lies,
That come true in the dark dreams
Of restless lives, proving
Nothing dies.

So, listen, my darling sweet:
Waves may eat away the shore,
Toss the boat, and break the oar,
Tall mountains may pierce the sky,
Clouds may hide peaks from the eye,
Rivers may dry and sands may melt;
Only *love* is deeply felt and dealt
In life and lore.

Moon's Sister

When the moon saw your proud, uplifted face,
Majestically gazing at the twinkling stars above,
She asked of them, "Is there some other moon
Down there on the earth, attired in silver lace."

"Oh yes," they replied. "She is a terrestrial damsel,
Graced by gods with a luminous face and form,
Extremely gifted, as you, with wit and charm."
The moon cried, "Then she must be no Jezebel."

"Most certainly not," they chimed, with reason:
"She is gracious of manner, made of your beams,
A happy denizen of the earth, but it also seems
She does change her form with time and season.

"In the mornings she rises as sun from the ocean,
Her hair spread in all directions as rays in motion.
In the evenings, she dances among the tall trees,
Rustling their leaves, arching the sky with ease.

"In the spring, she becomes the lily of the valley,
With white, sensuous little flowers, eager to dally.
In the summer, she assumes the form of a peach,
With delicate fuzz and fragrance, ready to teach

"The art and craft of love, like her cousin Venus.
In the fall, she turns into a crisp, rosy-juicy apple.
In the winter she turns into a kitten most supple.
O dear moon, your sister isn't only of one genus."

66

Bulbul[1]

A bulbul was hiding in a lush green bush
(Unaware of her ruffled toosh[2]),
Turning a merry song into a proper trill
For her lover with a gorgeous frill.

The bulbul's lover was in another bush.
He saw his sweetheart's raised toosh.
His heart beat faster, his legs made a push
To her perch with a swishshsh.

Seeing her lover so close and near,
"Oh dear!" she cried, "I am glad you are here.
Hold me to your breast, my dear,
Let us make a love dance without fear."

They kissed and cooed on the beams of sun.
They puffed their feathers in sheer fun,
Then trilled and thrilled the bushes in unison;
When happily done, they flew as one.

1 A Persian song bird (*Luscinia golzii*)
2 A short gown (here, of feathers)

Le Mina Bird

Pretty, sweet le Mina bird,
Your melody was heard
By the king and the clown,
In the forest and the town,
Where you sang the song
Of lasting love all day long.

Far away you may soon fly,
But the echo of your song
Will remain and never die
Or disappear from my eye.
It will bring great joy to all
In spring, summer, and fall.

Though immortal you are not,
But surely in your soft melody
Is a heavenly spirit so wrought.
It fills my heart in pure ecstasy,
Lifting my hopes beyond the sky,
As if the heaven were just nigh.

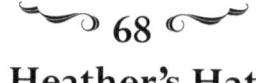

Heather's Hat

Oh Heather, oh sweet Heather,
Your jaunty hat needs a feather;
Tomorrow, we'll go together,
A pheasant's feather to gather.

In the deep woods we will go,
Where fragrant flowers grow,
Where sparkling rivulets flow,
Like fireflies in the night glow.

In this place, the summer heat
Is cooled by a breath so sweet,
From a bed of heather so neat,
It makes hearts together beat.

There, in the perfumed glen,
The painted pheasants roam,
Strutting under an airy dome,
Dappled with gold, as in Rome,
Proud birds of nature's tome!

Pheasants can be quite onerous.
I will beg them to be generous,
To give a tail feather beauteous
For my lady's hat, to honor us.

Seeking Atonement

Talking with you this morning
Was like walking on thin ice,
Which comes with its own price:
Each step sounding a warning.

Your recently listed accusations
May be either true or false,
But are these not clear calls
Of anguish that can't be scoffed?

My love, you feel most injured,
Lied to, and cleverly fooled,
Unjustly caught and spooled;
But these feelings are conjured.

Yet I can't ignore how you feel;
Therefore I must quickly own
My responsibility and atone,
Kneel, and pray for you to heal.

If you think my love is a big lie,
Then I have failed to show,
Or you have seen in me a foe;
These silly imaginings must go.

They don't do justice to reason
Or to our feelings for each other
But reflect our ruffled emotions
That can't be called treason.

Believe it or not, I'm concerned
About your emotional state
And wrestle daily against hate
Not to let it embitter our fate.

Your Sorrow

Your sorrow surpasses mine
More than you allow me to see;
Yet its quickly fading shadow
Is clearly visible to me.

I too am sorrowing for you,
With love – unbounded and free;
But my sorrows, in your absence,
Find no expression to relieve me.

You and I occupy the same space,
But we measure time differently;
You see the *past* in your *future*,
Forgetting the *present* intently.

The difference between you and me
Is not as large as it seems to be.
You take the *present* for granted;
I see it as a haven for you and me.

Stop raking the ashes of past history.
Stop aching for the future mystery.
We can't bend the time's two ends,
So let's enjoy what the *present* lends.

This world is not a stifling place
Deserving our dismay or derision,
But our thankfulness, for the solace
That *time* provides without omission.

Time is not a river that flows by
Under our wakeful or sleeping eye;
It is a rainbow of feelings in space,
Carrying us along in its embrace.

So why should we grieve or sorrow
For the past errors or the future fears
When *today* our hearts are still beating
And the gifts of love and life greeting?

Desperation

Tick, tock went the willful clock.
Testy thoughts streamed in a flock
And kept me awake until the dawn,
When black dew settled on the lawn.

Clop, clop pounded my tired heart.
Every irregular beat gave me a start.
The night grew darker and very long;
I couldn't even hum a rag of a song.

Click, click, you go shod in the green
Sandals, hugging your planter's arch.
With uplifted heals you boldly march
Over the cast glances— gallant or mean.

Oh! your graceful steps waste no time.
They perform a dance in perfect rhyme
To the admiring eyes and choked sighs
From those who give you new highs.

Darling! it is now very hard to hide.
There is no way out but for us to abide
By our human nature, so we may find
What goes on in your and my mind!

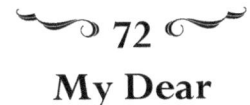

My Dear

When you tell me,
"I *was* yours,"
Or
"You *had* me,"
My head aches,
My heart breaks.

What is the sense
In using *past tense*?
When the fact is
I *am* yours forever
And have you always
In my heart, I swear.

The *present tense*
In my heart's speech,
I pray, should reach
Your faltering sense
That I am still hoping
To be with you hence.

But if you have given
Me up for some other
To seek some solace,
I'll tell my heart to hush
And beg you not to blush
For having said – seriously,
"I will always love you."

Desire

If
you're still
on his hook,
then let him reel
you ashore, sans grief,
you'll breathe once again
through your palpating gills
to your cardio-vescular relief;
and shun your fear and disbelief.

But!
if you're the one
angling,
and he slipped
off the tangled line,
then try again and again,
for you've so much to gain
from swiftly landing him flat
on your luscious, mossy bank.

Yet!
one way or other,
even better,
it will fill the cup
of your pent-up desire,
for the sensations honed,
but long enough postponed,
that fevered your brain a lot
and broke my craving heart.

Make a Choice

How can I doubt
When you say,
"No, I have not."
For don't we know
That you simply can't,
For the darned reason
That you may be caught,
And so ought.

Some like it hot,
But you like it warm;
In superficial pleasures
You find peculiar charm.
As butterflies to flowers
Do adoringly advance,
To imagined lovers,
You tap dance.

Just try to distinguish
Red flame from the blue:
First is easy to extinguish;
Second heats you so true.
So make your choice
On the color blue;
Its intensity
Comes through.

You ain't no fool,
With looks so cool,
When we fully know
You don't mindlessly sow
Shriveled seeds of discontent
In hearts solely intent
On loving you,
Only you.

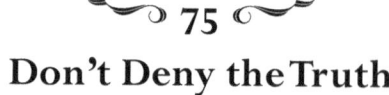

Don't Deny the Truth

You would do what you said you wouldn't,
Of this I had no doubt from the beginning.
The promise you made in this case couldn't
Be true, for a new love is always beckoning.

I didn't ask, require, or even expect of you
To give up your incessant longing for love,
Sought in pursuit of fame and of variety too.
So why wouldn't you take a new lover now?

You liked to be held from spring to winter,
Cuddled, kissed, rolled up and then down.
How can you now from these joys splinter
And not let down, for the other, your gown.

You and I used to climb walls to make love.
We wouldn't lie still till our lights went out.
The old lover gone, look for a new one now;
You will, otherwise, lose your charming clout.

So cling to your new love on the featherbed,
And hold him snugly in your tropical groves,
Whispering words that can't be openly said
But swell the torrid waves crashing in droves.

Don't deny the truth its due place in your life.
You deserve to be worshiped by gods, not men.
Get your druthers and try – be some god's wife.
You'll be free to glide, and freer to slide, then.

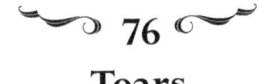

Tears

Tears — shed for shame or sorrow,
Or of pain from a crushing blow,
Or for a promised joy tomorrow
Look alike, but differ in their glow
When seen in the light of feelings,
Which accompany their flow.

Tears of shame have a scarlet hue
Of pain and sorrow — a shade blue.
Yet, all in all, as they slip and fall
From the laden eyes and eyelashes
Down my love's face — in a squall,
My heart sinks and crashes.

When I see the ruby drops swelling
In her sideways-looking, misty eyes,
I promptly join her with my cries.
For the guilt feeling she has defies
All remedies — medical or otherwise;
For she is a captive to sweet lies.

But if her tears have a bluish touch
And fall like a cascading stream,
I don't know for sure, but this much:
That in her soul some sorrow screams,
Hard to let go, but harder to keep;
Then I offer her my shoulder to weep.

Deception & Jealousy

Is this what you wanted all along?
Hush my voice and mute my song!
Erase my memory, held too long!
Push me to where I don't belong!
If so, then whom did you wrong.
Me! I bet you aren't that strong.

Was it fair to have fooled me thus?
When there was no reason to bus
Your charm to all in the omnibus,
Casting lusty eyes without any fuss,
Reaching out like a hungry octopus,
Piling brazen shame on both of us?

Scheming is your trade, O wily one,
Dreaming of others is your only fun,
Preferring the married — well done —
Equipped with a small or a big gun!
(You do quickly understand a pun.)
You are always ready to be undone.

There is a way to save your red face:
Carry it neatly packed in a suitcase.
Drop it quietly at your lover's place,
And let him figure out how to erase
The dark red lies that lace your face
And save you from further disgrace.

Contention

You accuse me of cursing you and your clan,
Mercilessly destroying your ego and élan,
While I know how brazenly you kept calling
Me and my friends by names quite appalling.

But is there any truth in words said in anger?
Is there any merit in letting them linger?
Whose victory is there in fighting forever?
Whose defeat is there in condoning never?

Over and over we repeat the same old line,
Like a broken record that was once fine;
But now the time to discard it has come,
Our injured pride mustn't make us dumb.

What purpose is there in holding a grudge?
What point is there in never ever to budge?
What honesty is there in not being fair?
What beauty is there when no one is dear?

You turn some simple words on their head,
Drawing meanings never intended or said.
Your hurt feelings bring up long-gone issues,
Then your eyes hide behind tears and tissues.

I was then, as now, seeking a life with you,
Of love and peace, with complications few,
Which are easy to handle, but not the kind
That leave you drained and perplexed to find.

Metamorphosis

I find I am changing little by little each day.
Metamorphosis of some kind! You may say,
Of the mind more than my body, by the way.

Be not beguiled. I look the same as yesterday,
Yet I recognize myself less and less each day;
A cursed knife has cleft me in a strange way.

She was like a mirror to my mind and soul;
One look from her eyes made me whole.
Oh, I placed all my hopes in a crystal bowl.

She was quite lovely, loving, kind, and just,
But battered by a mindless war – if you must
Know the truth – turning a diamond into dust.

For she was torn by savage notions of love,
Placing love of love and freedom far above;
This tossed her from man to man anyhow.

Her wandering spirit could not distinguish
How her lovers would be driven to anguish
If she couldn't her inane desires extinguish.

Whenever she set her heart on just any one,
Her love dance began with the morning sun
In stringed overtures until the prize was won.

Flirtation would start with a genial discourse,
With colleagues, clients, and guests, of course,
Provoking a romantic interest with silent force.

She knew how to make them depend on her.
Using her charm and office, she made them
Settle cases on terms she alone could offer.

I watched her clever pattern from the tower
And confronted her delicately in our bower,
But my protestations had no effect or power.

I couldn't stop her from her destructive ways,
Thus I hated and loved her on alternate days,
And this process pushed my mind into a haze.

The creeping weeds in my brain I couldn't trim.
Doubt filled my reckoning vessel to the brim.
My heart grew sore, my mind wretchedly grim.

With my grief growing day by day, a big change
Came over me — a change frighteningly strange,
In that my mind wandered over a bizarre range.

The solid rock I stood on went soft and spongy.
The rose bushes in the backyard turned mangy.
My reason went up and down like on a bungee.

I combed the murky waters of stagnant pools,
Flew into the dark clouds tethered to spools
Of horrid ideas that swirl in the heads of fools.

But nowhere did I find a single crumb of truth
That would guide me home as it did poor Ruth,
So I remained trapped in my own foggy booth.

Now, as I am trying to crawl out of my space,
I sense my mind is broken and bound in a case
Similar in substance to a beetle's body and face.

The end of my transformation isn't easy to tell.
My incoherent thoughts can't escape my shell,
But I am trying best to break free from this hell.

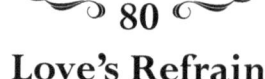

Love's Refrain

Why have I placed my happiness
In your hands
And kept my hopes in the haziness
Of arid lands?

Why do I crave for summer breeze
In winter freeze,
Search for green in the sapless trees
That do not please?

Why do I wait for the sun to shine
On the cloudy days,
When it is the rain that is just fine
In so many ways?

Why do I thirst for a word from you,
Who is always busy
With tight schedules of multiple hue
That make me dizzy?

Why not place my heart elsewhere
To provide it some rest?
Why not quench it in a pool of fire
Where life is toasted best?

Why not!

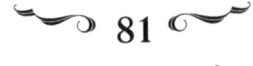

Love's Demise

Alas, we have reached an impasse!
You by your reckoning and reason,
I by mine; neither willing to unmask
Self-deception and pride in the season
Of fall, when the apples ripen and ask
The arch serpent its poison to pass.

Yes, we have caused hurt and pain
To each other, but it is hard to grasp:
Why we can't break free and rise again
From the cave of shadows to vivid light,
Where eagles soar high without a gasp,
And larks their wings and songs regain!

But is it now possible to easily resume
The same old exciting song and presume
That our Eden's gate is not too far away,
But lies within easy reach of love's way?
Somehow our destiny's map has changed,
Its colors and contours artfully rearranged.

So here we are now – witlessly reaping
The bitter fruit of betrayal, and weeping
To wash our minds clean of life's deceit,
Yet unwilling to confess or admit defeat,
Out of fear, self-preservation, or conceit.
When truth dies, love can't be speaking.

Bitten by Light

I tend to see a light
Where there's none,
So little for heart's delight,
So much for reality shun.

You had trained me to believe
Every word you casually said,
But the cards in your sleeve,
I found, were with faces red.

How can I read between the lines
When the writing is overwritten
And the red ink starkly shines
Its light on a heart sorely bitten?

Differences

Why do you like me?
I am not your kind,
I am not that kind.
You like leisure and love,
With all their passing flavors;
I salute life — the arching bow,
Stringing it with mundane labors,
Wetted in boiling blood of love.

Why do you want me
When you know it?
Candles can't be lit
On the stormy shores of doom,
Which beckon me to face soon
Myriad fears that quietly bloom,
Even after the passing of a typhoon.
Why do you crave the waning moon?

I may seem more than one,
Combining images of them all,
Like a broken mirror reflecting the sun;
It's my scattered fragments you recall.
But I am overlain by earth and snow,
Composting with the fallen leaves,
Yet you imagine or pretend to know
That I am hiding under your eaves.

You are like a lightning,
Streaking the night in a flash,
A bright corolla quickly opening,
Pouring out its streams of scent
To drown the unsuspecting traveler
In the sweet opiates of dreams—
Lodged in the sleepy eyes of the reveler
That wake him by his own silent screams.

You are like no one I have seen:
Loving, but combing the dark streets
With a thirsty tongue and senses keen,
Licking salty popsicles for sweet treats,
Gulping down adorations and moans
In rocking cars and on telephones.
I can't blind my eyes or plug my ears,
Or wash my wounds in acid tears.

I loved you once to distraction;
Wide and deep was my attraction.
My prayers kept the stars gazing,
But all this madness was amazing.
Then I heard the snakes by my feet hissing,
While we were bloodying our lips kissing;
I felt an invisible finger jab at my chest,
And a voice in my heart said the rest.

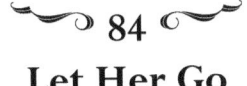

Let Her Go

She has decided to go.
That much I know,
For water must flow
Or else icicles grow.

Yet I mutely wonder:
Why this silly blunder?
Is it resident in their gender?
Why no light, but only thunder!

Neither fine mist nor rain
In the eyes seemingly in pain
Give any pause to entertain
A doubt or refrain.

A smile on their face
Is often hard to trace
To its meaning or case,
Crocheted in delicate lace.

Should I stop or let her go?
Give a chance for a miracle to show!
No, my heart, you better learn to grow
Peaceful, and let her wonder to and fro.

Goodbye

I lie awake
All night a lot,
In my cold bed burning hot,
Asking, why did you cut the tie
Without saying a goodbye.

We were like
Two billing doves,
Two wings of a bird,
Two peas in a pod;
That is why it is so damn hard.

It's vain to feign
That "I am not deeply hurt,"
Or "I don't care anymore,"
Or even "This too shall pass."
I wish I could say it, but I can't, alas.

For that isn't how I feel,
And I suppose, neither do you.
But it's true: you broke the deal,
So how can I simply repeal
A bitter fact with a feel-good lie.

So let me see
From your point of view
And imagine what you would say:
"I didn't want to leave,
But you gave me no sign to believe."

In my innocence,
Which was of essence
To our coexistence,
I kept hoping we to each other belonged;
But your roving eyes proved me wrong.

So why don't I
Get a shard of sleep in my eye?
But keep on tossing and turning
In my cold bed, burning hot,
When there are better things to sort.

Search Your Heart

Touch your heart and you will see
Clearly in your mind's discerning eye
That you've judged me differently
Since we exchanged a goodbye.

Until then, I was the only one
Whose company you wouldn't shun,
For then we had a life you so craved,
And every danger you so gladly braved.

Now you avoid me, as if I am a pain
In your eye that can't open or shut.
Is it because we have together lain,
And now you with another cohabit?

I don't hold this a bit against you,
For everyone does the same shit;
But you were among those few
Who proclaim they don't fall in it.

If your conscience is hurting you,
Where did you get it all at once?
Or is it the fear of your new beau,
That he too may call you a dunce.

My dear, you don't have to change
Your old tactics to please your beau.
It'll make you stranger than strange
And pull down your cover and show.

So, please, don't judge me differently,
Or your own self – for it is what it is:
Human beings tied to desires endlessly
Search for new pleasures constantly.

Poor Return

You gave me joy; I gave you sorrow,
With vague promises of tomorrow,
Prolonging them both endlessly.

You gave me love; I gave you tears,
Which submerged me in a sea of fears
And unnecessary cares – senselessly.

You gave me hope and reason to live;
I squandered it all in moments so few,
Like water running out of a rusty sieve.

You tried to spread happiness over all;
But I was bound by my history to fall
On the thorns of life, poisoned by gall.

You saw beauty in perfect harmony;
I remained captive to useless duty,
Drowning myself in mere absurdity.

Why were we so poorly fashioned?
Why were we so foolishly frightened?
Why were we so damn easily broken?

If we had eschewed our human frailty
And carefully measured our reality,
Our dreams would have come true.

Life's sorrows may seem to have no end,
For they greet you at each bloody bend,
But we shouldn't give up our hope easily.

Undoing

"Those pretty wrongs that liberty commits,
When I am absent from thy heart."
-William Shakespeare, "Sonnet 41"

If I could see you once again!
Not where we had met or been before:
The first time, when we fell in love,
Or the last, where we missed our shore,
Or where the demons of desire roam;
But there where the air is crisp
And kissed by love's mist.

There, witnessed by a clear stream,
Flowing over the bedrocks of my dream,
Through a meadow where buttercups are ready
To fill our cups with honeyed cream;
I would open my heart to open your eyes.

Near that glistening stream of pure reason,
In the sweetly flowering season of thought,
I could, my love, easily un-guise the treason
That sundered our bonded souls apart,
Just like a hammer breaking a rock.

Alas! it was only our egos' doing,
Seeking wantonly a way out from losing
Our false sense of freedom, liberally oozing
In all directions, out of an endless craving
For attention that became our undoing.

Ask, "Can freedom-seeking undo love?"
Yes, if we confuse freedom with liberty
And keep stretching the latter too far
Without giving a thought or pause;
Then such liberty becomes the cause.

There is now enough reason to un-cause
Our senselessly tragic undoing, because
Life without you isn't worth a dime,
So let us rejoin in one perfect rhyme
The scattered words of our poem.

I Remember

I remember, I remember
Your each gold-minted word
Uttered just once,
But twice heard.
First, when it hit my resonating drum,
Leaving me momentarily numb,
Then when it reached my heart
And woke me up with a start.

I remember, I remember,
What you quietly said,
Jumping off the bed,
On that glorious morn of May:
"I love you so,
Please don't go."
I couldn't believe my ears or heart
Or heed this wondrous thought.

The seed of sorrow thus sown,
Quickly grew into a rank weed
Nourished by tears of resentment,
Mistrust, and badly bruised sentiment!
Puzzling as it may seem,
Our love was like a wild dream,
Indeed, a torrent that cried aloud
For truth – hiding in a dark cloud.

I distinctly remember
How sorrowfully we said our adieus,
Assuring each other of exchanging news.
But the lamps of love in our eyes
Could not be dimmed by our cries
Of despair that fogged the chamber,
Still shining your amber eyes,
Which I will always remember.

The memory of our painful parting
Will remain in my soul till its departing.

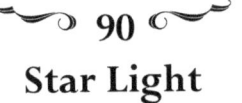

Star Light

When I lie under the canopy of night
It isn't to read or count the stars
But to invite their fading light
Into my heart that chars
Ready to extinguish and crash
Like a last dying ember on its ash

Oh, let that Delphian dream come
And hold me in its hypnotic trance
Easing my tearing tension some
With a heart-warming glance
From your emerald eyes
To sleep without sighs

I miss you very much
Your smell and touch
Far away from my reach
These memories can't beseech
You to be generous with your dole
Though they are imbued in my very soul

Express Letter

Yes, I am still crazy about you
Even after our byes
Uttered in sighs
Tears in eyes
And cries
So long ago and after so many tries
To resurrect our love and lives

I still miss you day and night
Holding in my heart
Your loving heart
Only to smart
With art
That keeps me thinking a lot
What I sought and what I got

How can I deny what was true
Then – even as now
Adoring you so
O angel blue
It is true
I find it hard to live without you
For persons like you are but few

I can't resurrect my happiness
In such a loneliness
Much sadness
It's madness
I confess
So I'm sending this letter express
But need to find your new address

Dreams

You come and go
In my dreams as you please.
Is it just to show
How you can tease?

What do you find
In being so unkind
To a man sleeping blind,
Yanking him out of his mind?

Last night, in my sleep,
I saw you by my side asleep;
My heart took a joyous leap,
Alas! this dream I couldn't keep.

I opened my eye,
But you weren't there;
Your stealthy flight all senses defy,
Waking up only an unknown fear.

Bare feet you roam in
All the corridors of my mind,
Like a Hindu quietly uttering Aum,
Appealing to a deity to be very kind.

I am under no illusion
That your visitations speak of love;
You want to keep me in that delusion
Until you purge me out of your mind.

Peace Comes Gently

"Hope it's a lovely day,"
She said,
Waking up from her bed,
Slowly inhaling the fragrant breeze
Coming from a stand of sweet peas
In the backyard — blooming gay

On this beautiful day.
She put on a silk gown
And stepped down
To her redwood deck,
Enclosed by a black-painted iron guard,
Overlooking the garden in the backyard,
Where the sweet peas and roses in bloom
Were beaming to dispel her gloom.

She looked at the flowers
Wistfully, recalling
How he had planted them,
The rootstocks and seeds on his knees,
After she and he had become pledged lovers
And given each other the keys to unlock
Their desires and mysteries.

But now he wasn't there
To hold her close or near;
They had separated out of fear
Of each other's cheating tendency
That poisoned their trust and intimacy.
They seemed to have done nothing wrong,
Yet suspicion rooted and grew strong.

The separation was hard to bear,
For their love was not an ordinary affair.
They had dared and sacrificed too much,
So they suffered in silence day and night.
The freedom they'd sought became a fright,
As an albatross round the neck,
Bringing fear and gloom.

Gone from her world
Was the thrill and comfort of his love
(The wind under the wings of the dove);
And he too was mercilessly hurled
On a thorny ground with his hands bound;
But both buried their heads in the sand
And ate the dust of their love by hand.

As she looked at the flowers below,
Trying hard to soak in their glow,
In her broken heart, beating slow,
She felt his spirit magically flow
From the garden into her whole frame
(Body and mind and soul — all together)
Bringing her peace, whispering her name.

The Passion to Keep

I must my petty passions set aside:
Forget the roses blooming in my yard,
Where I spend my whole day to hide
From myself, my neighbor, and God;
Surely, I must this passion set aside.

As for the books that burn my eyes
Through the long hours past midnight,
When these romances I try to fantasize,
Just, by proxy, to draw a little delight;
Surely, I must this passion set aside.

On the wet rainy days, I like watching
Raindrops beating time on the leaves,
Making their dance quite eye-catching.
Watching this, my heart gently heaves,
But I must this passion too set aside.

These silly passions of mine helped me
Hasten the flow of days and nights,
So I could sooner my real passion see,
Unfolding in all her dazzling lights,
Like a well-lit harbor nestled in a lee.

Now I have received this intimation
That she is coming back to live with me
In my lonely aboard, which is needed
Not only for her to take the reins again
But to undo the guilt of forsaking me.

She has been my only love and passion,
Consuming every drop of attention,
Radiating essence, as a cashmere rose.
From her mind, loving visions arise
To her voluptuous lips that surprise
And transport you to a heavenly isle,
Where the sun plays hide and seek
Through the moving clouds – to peek
At her sinuous form and emerald eyes,
Reaching out for passionate highs.

This is the only passion I want to keep.

Do the Dead Talk?

It is often said, the dead don't talk.
They smolder under earth and rock
Or go down the river in burnt ash
And vanish after a brief splash.
But I wonder if it's completely true.
And do the dead also hold this view?

No, it can't be even partially correct,
For we know some do fully resurrect.
And I have heard myself the dead speak
From wherever they be, if we avidly seek
The memories – of those we truly loved,
Held in the faded threads of our shroud.

Some of the dead let their persona heave
Through a rich legacy of deeds they leave
In science, philosophy, commerce, or art.
But I am not pursuing this line of thought.
Here I am speaking of the sensory fare
That the dead offer to the unaided ear.

In the winter of my soul, when I clean
The ash-filled fireplace to light, I just lean
To hear the quaint swishing sound of air,
Bringing the many whisperings of my dear
Departed love distinctly to my thirsty ear,
And her lovely voice I do once again hear.

A number of intimate letters quietly rest
In a locked compartment of my old chest.
When I open them again and begin to read,
I hear her voice flow with each line, indeed,
Intoning each word in its expressed feeling
That I may have missed in my first reading.

In the spring season, I see her on the deck,
Watching me pruning the roses and plucking
The older ones whose color time has faded.
I hear her calling me in a voice too jaded,
Admonishing not to cut the fading flower,
For it has still a life left to charm its lover.

A Vision

"What fortitude the soul contains,
That it can so endure
The accent of a coming foot,
The opening of a door!"
Emily Dickinson

What should I do!
When I hear once again,
after the stream has dried up,
leaving a trickle of memories,
the familiar sound of her feet,
muffled by the soft slippers,
smelling of bruised roses,
outside my door?

Yes, we're once together,
sweetly killing each other
with the insanity of love;
but she's no more now,
and I live with my fate
in the womb of pain,
waiting to see her
face-to-face again.

So, what should I do
when I don't know
if I am awake or in a dream
seeming to sense her close by?

Just stop breathing to hear well
or inhale the perfumed air to tell
if she is really there, still hesitating
to own me again — with a kiss to kill!

I'm too confused but refuse to believe
that she doesn't want my pain to relieve;
so I jump from my bed and rush to the door.
As I open it, she imperially steps onto my floor.

Love beyond Death

My thirst has congealed
On my lips — a stone I see;
I fell in your river and healed,
But came out still thirsty!

The arrows from your eyes
Pierced my heart's sanctuary,
Lifting my soul to the skies,
Blown by your cute archery.

So many have admired you,
But they all remained alive
And fully able to continue
Striving for the honey hive.

Now, since you have killed me,
I am entombed in darkness,
Begging death to let me see
You again — my claim to press.

As moths love to see a flame,
Wherein they burn and die,
My love for you is no game,
As death and I together lie.

Your Silence

The day has folded,
The church bells chime,
You haven't spoken
For a long time.

The snow has melted,
Bare ground meets the eye,
Your prolonged silence
Makes me cry.

The daffodils are swaying
In the spring breeze,
My heavy heart is still
In the deep freeze.

Why do you hold me
In your invisible arms,
When you are distantly
Withholding your charms?

A moonless night
Is now upon me;
Sleepless, lonely I will be,
Unable to touch you or see.

This world will go on,
No matter what we do.
My life has shortened
For want of you.

Love's Labor Lost

There is a vase-like jar
On my kitchen shelf,
Full of sweet-scented honey
Stolen from a hive of busy bees.
They had built it in my backyard.

The jar reminds me
Of my bygone honey –
With slim waist and syrupy eyes,
Quiet, funny, and very sunny –
In love, till we broke apart.

Like me, the bees are
In turmoil, quite aghast
At their love's labor lost;
Buzzing angrily, they are now
Vainly looking for the cause.

Loss of labor, money, or honey
To creatures – big or small –
Causes injury that's visible to all,
Except the Wall Street climbers,
Whose fortunes rise and fall.

Shadow of Memories

"When to the seasons of sweet silent thought
I summon up remembrances of things past,
I sigh the lack of many things I sought."
-William Shakespeare, "Sonnet 30"

Under the shadow of my memories,
I bask, lounge, doze, and fall asleep,
Entering a dream world of ecstasies,
Where, fully awakened, I then keep
Flipping the pages of my history,
Some still legible in black and white,
Others faded into grays of mystery,
But, all combined, beguiling insight.

Yet no page so vital or to this equal,
For it keeps me wondering why
My eye fell on that priceless jewel,
Which, on credit, I couldn't buy,
And lacking courage, couldn't steal.
This jewel was no other but her love,
Which I coveted and wanted to seal,
But, to devil and death, lost the deal.

Part III

Reflections on Light

Light

"When He shines, everything begins to shine.
Everything in this world reflects His light."
-Mundaka Upanishad

"In the cave of the Heart, the True I
Radiates alone with a subtle Light
The one essence shining forth without defect —
Blissful consciousness of Being."
-Oleg Mogilever, "Inquiry into the 'I'"

The Path

There
In sorrow
And humility
Lies the secret
Of evolving strength
And unfolding wisdom,
Harnessed by perseverance;
As shown by a wise Nazarene.

This path leads to our freedom
From the grim fetters of desires
That tie us to the yoke of bondage,
Causing us an irreversible damage.
Stuck in the wet, miry furrow, the ox,
With his uplifted eyes, humbly thanks
his Maker
For the downpour that cooled his back,
Giving some respite from his burdens.

Pulling thus the life's drag thru time,
Stop periodically to thank and pray,
So that your fortitude may not flop,
And your resolution doesn't snap.

This process ensures restoration
Of peace in your weary mind,
Stamina in you tired body,
And light in your soul.
As you are restored,
You will achieve
True wisdom
And freedom.

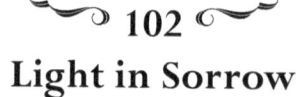

Light in Sorrow

In sorrow abides the kingdom
Of steadily evolving endurance,
Slowly ripening perseverance,
And gently unfolding wisdom.

But they need sacrifice to mature,
Pain and suffering first to endure,
As the misshapen nugget of gold
Takes heat and hammer to mold.

Ask, "What gain is there in pain
And suffering?" Let me explain:
While pain summons endurance,
So suffering incubates patience.

Pain is a stern teacher of tolerance,
Suffering: an antidote to arrogance.
On losing a loved one, we sorrow,
Then recover from it tomorrow.

Pain and suffering have a limited span.
They are diffused by time and élan,
By the painfully gained experience
And our wisdom and perseverance.

"Everything existing in the universe
is the fruit of chance and necessity."
-Democritus

As the distant star sheds its bright light
and becomes dim,
As the journeying meteorite in its flight
burns at earth's rim,
As the flowing stream erodes the solid rock
on its own bed,
As the icy wind lifts the swift flying hawk
and lays it dead,
We all are solitary specks of luminous dust
floating in space,
Not so formidable that time's bloodlust
can't easily erase.

So in cosmos lie together *being* and *emptiness*
for some strange reason
Unknown to mortals, but surely evolving
beyond trust or treason.

If that is the order, decree, and destiny
of all there is,
Then what holds us back from an epiphany,
for that too is His?
Why not drink, devour, and conquer time
and its tortuous history?
And why not stop time's mournful chime,
its unending *mystery*?

We are told to use *free will* to figure a way out
that would be right;
But none reach the empyrean height without
sacrifice and divine light.

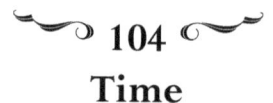

Time

"Devouring Time, blunt thou the lion's paws,
And make the earth devour her own sweet brood,
Pluck the keen teeth from the fierce tiger's jaws,
And burn the long-lived phoenix in her blood."
-William Shakespeare, "Sonnet XIX"

Time! you swift steed of blinding light,
Straight and sharp as Apollo's arrow bright,
You fly forth without any hindsight or rest,
Piercing cosmic dust and the human breast.

No one can see you fly by, or catch or hold.
You skip quickly by seconds that can't be told.
You leap by eons in steps immeasurably bold
And watch the world in glances divinely cold.

You think you are quite uniform in your stride;
In your measured steps you take immense pride.
But see: a lover finds an hour too short and shy;
The ailing child finds it too long to sleep or cry.

You cast strange spells that are too hard to tell.
You are famed to heal sorrow, yet you compel
The bereaved to stand up and swallow his grief.
You tease and torture, then restore us – in brief.

Time! are you truly the web and warp of space?
Its intangible dimension, its divine cord or lace?
Be whatever thou art, but as I listen to my heart,
Without my *being* you wouldn't stir, or start.

Somber Thoughts

O! somber thoughts, raise your head
From the murky depths of oceanic floor,
With uplifting power of volcanic force,
And let your clear voice heavenward soar.

You have remained patiently submerged
Under old Neptune's trident for too long,
Lending your words a briny-bitter taste,
And, seemingly, on your lips a sad song.

Grave and melancholy you may seem,
But your ideas do have a sanguine edge.
Colored thus, they do often unsettle us;
But, in truth, to truth you point and pledge.

Dark and drab your appearance may seem
To those who witness you from outside,
But in your thoughts, deep meaning I see,
For they all cant and vagueness kick aside.

A serious purpose they bring to life:
In demanding prudent actions from us,
Somber though they are, so is our strife.
So why shouldn't we our wants confess?

O! somber thoughts, raise your head;
Proclaim the purpose for your existence,
For I know you goad us to move ahead
With courage and wisdom and persistence.

Human Folly

"Know then thyself, presume not God to scan,
The proper study of mankind is Man.
Placed on this isthmus of a middle state,
A being darkly wise and rudely great."
-Alexander Pope, "Essay on Man, Epistle II"

You of myriad woes seem to be seeking
The lightning that sunders the night
And, in a flash, reveals the jagged knife
Buried deep in your soul – illumined by light.

Consumed by endless desires that bred
A being so complex and shrouded in mystery,
You stand forlorn, in utter dread
Of the dark deeds that mark your history.

Oh man! you set yourself above the rest,
To conquer, change, and subdue all,
Hoping to remake nature as suits you best;
But you also let too much to slip and fall.

First of all, your fall from heaven's grace –
Ascribed to your disobedience to God[1]
Or ignorance of your kinship with All[2] –
Has darkly marked your face and race.

Was this your sin or God's design?
Or the work of a gift sublime – your ego,
Which was supposed to let you find your way
And assume a rightful place in the divine.

Your trust and perceived relief in *free will*
Is a two-edged sword; it lifts or drowns
Based on thy deeds of good or ill will,
While holding God's *will* to no account!

---

1 The Judeo-Christian veiw: disobedience to personal God and subsequent fall of Adam
2 The Hindu view: Avidya, meaning lack of knowledge of man's oneness with Brahman [Godhead]

When left to your own desires and devices,
You chose pride, aggrandizement, and greed;
Filled with lofty thoughts and base vices,
You swayed up and down like a thin reed.

Oh man! now you wonder what went wrong?
Why this war in your soul and the world around?
Why isn't there joyful dance, music, and song?
Why myriad woes remain with you all along?

Thickets and Pickets

Walk with me around this last bend;
Our difficult journey is about to end.
We have some more to sense and share:
New ideas and actions to test and dare.

Life's struggles have put us to moping,
But we must keep on searching, hoping
For a divine light to illumine our mind,
To free us from grim fetters of all kind.

Yes, we mope — for want of courage
To clear the dense thickets that encage
Our mortal ideas and actions in a vice.
These thickets bite and blind us in a trice.

We drive stakes and pickets of all kind
In the willing ground of our raw mind,
Then we avidly search around to find
Other ideas or actions that seem to bind

And jive with ours, securely underlined.
This inflates our ego and makes us blind
To opposite ideas that may also hold true
And be similarly impossible to disprove.

So, by our own making, picket by picket,
We find ourselves in a blinding thicket
Of ideas and actions that amount to naught,
While we keep on insisting they ought.

How can we break their pernicious hold?
We ask and ask till we grow very old.
But in our ardent search for a cool spring,
We must first jump through a fiery ring.

We could have taken this path before;
Stars would have led us to the shore.
It would be a much richer, happier time,
With innocence reigning, and no crime.

In our search for truth or beauty, we must
Seek harmony, not by racking logic's dust
To win a point by only its scientific force,
But by an intuitive feel for its fluid course.

So, my loving heart, walk with me
With courage and guiding reason,
That I may not ever forget to see
The truth and beauty in each season.

Heart and Soul

We talk of soul,
Believing
It dwells in us,
Not knowing
Its real origin,
Nature, or goal.

We use our mind
To explore
This world and more,
Without finding
What connects it
To our soul.

Then we ask
Our heart quietly,
"What should we do
To connect the two?"
The heart replies,
"Fill me with love,
And
That will do."

Ode to the Heart

"Thanks to the human heart by which we live,
Thanks to its tenderness, its joys, and fears,
To me the meanest flower that blows can give
Thoughts that do often lie too deep for tears."
-William Wordsworth, "Ode: Intimations of
Immortality from Recollections of Early Childhood"

O my heart! guide me with discerning light.
Lead my mind to find what is true and right
As I look far and see the *word* in my soul,
To write simply in praise of *You*, as my goal.

The land where the ancestors live and die,
Where civilizations flourish or in ruins lie,
There the human heart is a sacred ground
To mankind's ventures and victories found.

In the heart lies the garden of life and love,
The ground of intuition and know-how,
Where questions of being – who and how –
Are churned to find peace here and now.

The lands where hopes are sown to grow
And our fears weeded out – clearly show
How hate turns into love by a just reflection
Of light that hearts hold in contemplation.

Whereas the mind seems to know it all,
Its ability to sense being in no way small.
But trapped in the dented wheels of logic,
The mind is subservient to heart's magic.

The wondrous magic the heart supplies,
The rhyme and rhythm it quietly applies
To every part of the body and mind,
Gives us a vision of the unity in mankind.

In the lush garden of the heart, flowers don't die,
Leaves don't wither, and love sees eye to eye
With all, and anon, drawing close in unity
The scattered subjects and ideals of humanity.

In the heart where the soul quietly dwells,
Watching every move and mood that swells
Like a tide in the ocean, bidding one to act:
In a clear-honest-bold manner to resurrect.

The hopes that lie dormant in the mind
When nourished by heart's blood do find
A new strength to resurface and resurrect
And prompt the man not to give up, but act.

Visions in the mind assemble and dissemble
Like clouds herded by wind — in ensemble.
The beating heart spreads the fire of breath
To energize the body and mind until death.

The mind is abstract, the heart concrete,
Yet throbbing and full of feelings discrete.
The mind is too busy processing and turning.
The heart longs for true love and learning.

The mind dwells in a web of nervous matter,
Pushed and pulled, it can go helter-skelter,
But the good heart dwells in the land of love,
And its rhythms are watched from far above.

Visions of the extraordinary or prophetic kind
May arise from an uncommonly gifted mind,
But their actualization takes a brave heart
That is filled with grace and devotion a lot.

A dashing display of valor in love or war
Reflects quality of the hero's mind by far,
Yet without adequate courage in his heart,
Our hero wouldn't be able to stand or start.

We must fight our demons first in our heart,
Banish hate and fear before they begin to rot
The easily corruptible substance of our mind;
For what the heart can see, mind cannot find.

Waiting

My soul has wandered Ahead of me
In search of him,
Whom I am dying to see.

My heart is throbbing
Fast enough to kill me,
Yet my eyes are still
Waiting for him patiently.

My sensate body of clay
Is slowly giving away
To thirst and exhaustion,
But I must find my own way.

Yes, I may lose my body
And mind imminently,
But my hope is locked
In my soul permanently.

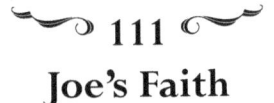

Joe's Faith

The road is too dusty and long,
Winding uphill through knotted roots
Of the old gnarled trees that throng
The rocky steep – hard to walk on.

Traveler Joe is tired and weary
Of the overhead pulsating sun,
Making his eyes teary with sweat,
Yet his climb is only half done.

The trees are bare and sapless –
Their leaves snatched by searing wind.
The stunted shadows fanning helplessly
Provide no shade or heat rescind.

But weary Joe keeps trudging on,
Breathing through his clenched teeth,
Straining the sinews of a heavy heart.
And he knows not what is in his lot.

Though exhausted, his will is strong,
Upheld by his firm faith in the Lord
That he'll see his Nina ere too long,
Before her spirit is recalled by God.

He knew she wasn't feeling too well,
For she had sent him an urgent word
To see her before she stumbled and fell
Under some spell – he hadn't heard of.

He keeps on marching to beat the death,
Which he presumes is nearing the bed
Where she is holding to her last breath,
To tell him what had remained unsaid.

The sun is down; the twilight has set.
Poor Joe is now near the cottage door,
Glad that he may have finally won the bet.
But, alas, his dear love is there no more.

He drops to his knees by the bedside,
Lowers his face to kiss her closed eyes,
Pulls her cold hands gently to his side,
Trying to wake her to life with his cries.

But she is now dead to his and her lies,
Lies that had once sustained his belief
That their love would soar in the skies
As his shackles came off — to his relief.

About a year back, Joe had been charged,
With his friend, Jon, for selling a drug.
But Jon, the sole culprit, had enlarged
His net — and framed Joe with a shrug.

While Joe was sentenced to 180 days,
Jon was free to do as he darkly chose:
He set up another intrigue like a maze
With silky lies, as is done only by foes.

Slumped in grief by dead Nina's bed,
Joe lifts her hands to kiss and console,
But finds therein a note written in red
And reads it twice to sink it in — whole.

Nina's note was straight as an arrow:
"Joe, your absence drove me to Jon,
Who saved me from my loneliness,
But left me pregnant and in this mess."

Joe was crushed as never ever before.
His faith in friendship, love, and God
Was being tested; he felt, therefore,
Urged to pray for Nina to his dear Lord.

He stood up gracefully to his full height
Near the footboard of cold Nina's bed,
Lifted his strong hands above his head And said,
"God, give my love your light."

Healing

The patient asked the healer, with a deep bow,
"What must be healed in sickness and how?"

"Body, mind, and soul," the healer replied.
"The body is the temple that nature supplied,
The mind its door, store, and reason's floor,
The soul its divine dweller, existent before."

The weary patient humbly ventured again,
"Body and mind with treatment may regain,
But why would soul, the indwelling divine,
Need healing? That I can't easily combine."

The sage replied, "Not for itself, but to regain
The lost connection between the three again;
So that the strings that play the melody best
Are in harmony and their discord put to rest."

At this the patient's eyes caught a bright gleam
From the light of wisdom — vital to redeem.

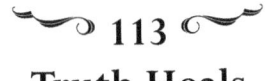

Truth Heals

There's little gain in hiding
What's clearly hanging out.
Bad faith can't be residing
In hearts that honesty spout.

When all is said and done,
There isn't much to guess,
Or look for a smoking gun
On a person ready to confess.

Truth and falsehood reside
Side by side in our minds,
Each side trying hard to undo
The other—simply to hide

Our inherent imperfection,
Making us fear the truth
More often than our lies,
Thus enticing us to mislead.

So, telling the plain truth,
When mistrust has grown
In our close relationships,
There trust can be re-sown.

Pleasure and Pain

Pleasure and pain come and go.
The marks they leave are so
Wrought-up with our ego
And the perseverance we show.

Life's joys and sorrows bear
Witness to our growing, rearing
Fortitude, like a mother caring,
Rocking her child out of its fear.

The joy of genuine pleasures
May lift us to touch the stars;
The pain of sorrows measures
Our will to break down the bars.

Grief and sorrow remind us how
Blind creatures feed and survive
In the murkiest waters somehow,
And how, by mercy, Job did revive.

Life's pleasures we must embrace,
For these are gifts given in grace
By the Providence who sees it all –
Our willed actions great or small.

Pleasure and pain come and go;
Both are fleeting in their flow.
Embrace pleasure gratefully so;
Embrace pain without stooping low.

You like it hot
For you can trot
With whatever you got
After daringly sought
With no thought
As your lot

I like it cold
For I'm told
It is a way wiser to hold
Than to be easily sold
On fool's gold
So I fold

An idea or belief
Held in a sheaf
Of molded leaf over leaf
Gives the soul no relief
But only grief
And disbelief

A love too warm
Folded in charm
May send bells of alarm
Warning of some harm
Twisting the arm
Has no form

A promise made
May quickly fade
In hot sun, not so in shade
Drying it on the table laid
In sly charade
Shouldn't jade

What do we gain
Other than pain
By the hot desires that strain
Our heads and hearts disdain
And duly drain?
It is so plain.

Innocence

You say you have lost your innocence!
Is it your credence or flagrance speaking
Or for some reason your heart aching
Unspeakably, so pricking your conscience?

How is it possible! When the snow is white
Even in the dark night, and the dewdrops shine
Like dazzling diamonds in the first rays of light,
Waking you up, like an angel in delight.

Is innocence an ornament worn and unworn?
Or like a feature on the body that gets torn —
As in the case of virgins raped and forlorn,
Then on the forked tongues of gossip borne!

Innocence is the sweetest fragrance of the soul
That graces some, if not all, whatever be its dole.
But no one has ever disputed its noble role;
Innocence has not only one meaning or goal.

It's a virtue much praised and pleasant to behold.
It makes childhood winsome, curious, and bold.
It makes youth on beauty, love, and promise sold.
It makes the aged bear their heavy crosses untold.

Innocence in humankind seeks equality for all —
In their treatment, toil, recompense, and reward.
Innocence must not ever be silenced for a gain,
Nor must it, for any whim or necessity, be slain.

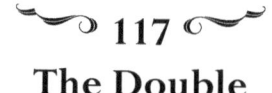

The Double

On an August afternoon,
With no reason to swoon,
As I was walking briskly down the lane
To meet a new lady friend from Tulane,
I figured my shadow was in some pain,
Trying to keep up in a reluctant strain.

For at every turn and bump in the lane
He visibly shrank or stretched or bent,
No matter how fast or slow I went;
He was plainly showing me his disdain.

My *own* shadow was acting most crazy,
Making me nervous ahead of my date
With this woman who was called Daisy;
And it was getting already far too late.

But I couldn't ignore my shadow's pain,
For it affected me too to no end or gain.
So I began to play the same trick again:
Cajoling him to calm down and remain

Vigilant to see the purpose of my quest
And not judge me by my nervous haste
Or whatever he thought a mere waste
Of time, but keep his patience at its best.

So I began to talk with him as earnestly
As I could about things not so mundane,
But which needed to come out honestly
To ease my raw conscience and his pain.

I asked my shadow, gently, "What ails thee?
Why do you shudder whenever I want to free
Myself of the fetters of fear that bind me?
My solitary existence I don't care to see."

On this, he lifted himself from the ground
And said, "You think your motives are sound,
But your choices have often had you so misled;
Your heart isn't in keeping with your head."

Just then, the sun went down,
And there rose the pale moon.

I Beseech You

Once again, I beseech you
Not to feel forlorn.
For a tree to be fruitful,
It can't bear when alone.

Good company is a boon
That doesn't dent solitude.
The bees visit a flowering tree
To bring it to fruit in plentitude.

This world, by its necessity,
Isn't alone or withdrawn
From other spheres of our galaxy,
But remains to them a paragon.

Don't be distraught, I implore,
By the attention you receive!
You will soon explore
The world, and duly perceive.

Power of Emotions

When emotions shape our thoughts,
Arising from our heads or hearts,
We simply assume our ideas are right;
This assumption bends our insight.

Emotions speak to us louder than logic,
Pulling us in with their power of magic,
As seen in conjugal love and religions:
Both invoking faith — with diligence.

But isn't faith based on an emotion
Inculcated with zeal and devotion?
Cleverly suggesting, "Not to question
But to believe and trust the equation;
Whether it is balanced square and fair,
For faith alone will all our doubts clear!"

So, working on our emotions thus,
We readily believe without any fuss,
Those who for their benefit love us,
Including the cult or religion we profess.

In this way, our thought is shaped
And in a full suite of emotions draped;
Yet we boast of being very objective
While our thoughts are just subjective.

Though pure logic should be our guide,
And in reasoning we should take pride,
Humans more often emotions like,
For they easily show our love or dislike.

Drawing a Line

Where do you draw the line
When the issues of heart or head
Burn your blood fuming red?
Or stretch your nerves too fine!

We face this dilemma often
In our real or imagined lives,
Yet this canker bug thrives,
Turning our heads into beehives.

Then our conscience is tested
In the dim caves of thought,
As a fly in a spiderweb caught:
Trying to escape is quickly wasted.

But lines can easily be drawn
In our broad mental space,
Assigning each issue its own place,
Where novel ideas may spawn.

Segregated thus, they won't collide
Or raise a din of cacophony
Or appear to be so deadly,
But certainly some solutions provide.

So where to draw a line?
No, not in the sand, air, or water
And not also in a state of anger,
But in your mind, where it will shine.

Second Chances

Sometimes happiness returns
Without any announcements,
Entering silently through a gate
That was once closed by ill-fate.

The hurts and dejections we feel
(That make us close our hearts)
Do sometimes miraculously heal,
And then a new happiness starts.

When the dust of our dreams
A cruel wind has blown away,
New dreams take their place
And hold us in their own sway.

Then time seems to stand still,
Holding us in its balmy embrace,
Quickening our heart's pace,
Restoring our hopes with grace.

Happiness we must surely claim,
But our sorrows too have an aim;
For to sense the sweetness of joy,
We should know our pain's ploy.

This cyclical design is revealed
In the workings of the universe,
Which pulsates like a live being,
Preserving its functions diverse.

So when happiness knocks again,
Be willing to open all the doors
Of your heart's empty chamber,
To let her in with her healing force.

Responsibility

You left it for me
To perceive and react
When I didn't see you
Unreasonably act.

I trusted you more
Than my own instinct,
For love was at its core,
So I never felt hoodwinked.

Now, if my blindness
Led you to squander
Your virtues to wickedness,
How can I your stains launder?

You are still perfect
In my blind eyes.
Now it's up to you to select
A way to turn away from lies.

Promenade

Two elegant rows of elm trees,
With sturdy trunk and green leaves
On all the extending branches borne,
A brick-lined promenade adorn.

Not narrow, curving, or short,
The promenade brings to life
The lovers walking abreast
In full display of their blissful art.

The lovers pause to admire
The two stands of rustling trees
That reach across and touch each other
Through the blue sky – and want to know

The truth that lies within all
And implores us to recall
What love needs most to be true and tall,
Besides an ardent heart to make its call.

The promenade through the trees
Provides a path to knowing this truth:
The leaves touching above tell us how to feel;
The light dancing below teaches us to kneel.

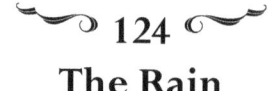

The Rain

The rain lost its angry bluster
Within an hour of beating hard
On the roses growing in a cluster
On a raised bed in my backyard.
The rain's fury didn't last long,
But its effect on me was strong.

The outburst of the untimely rain,
I felt, was not to my liking at all.
But when I saw the desolate plain,
Denuded, behind my garden wall,
It dawned on me that this storm
Would do more good than harm.

My neighbor's piece of dry land,
Where grasses struggle to grow,
Is just a wide bar of coarse sand
With not much to graze or mow
When clouds are dry or scarce,
And the sky sheds but few tears.

But when the rain blesses the land,
The emerald hidden in the sand
Comes alive as gay clover and grass
And gives the livestock a happy pass.
As this truth touched my heart,
I and my roses ceased to smart.

The Weeping Willow

The willow was weeping, yet
Keeping her green eyes fixed
On the rivulet running below,
Dreading when its rapid flow
Might slow down, then cease
Altogether; for the crops above
Need their lifeblood to keep
The farmers in their business.

There were other reasons too
For the willow's deep sorrow:
Her friend, the rainbow trout,
Would leave her for a stream
Running full to please its gills.
The doves too wouldn't come
To sit and sing on her boughs,
Pouring songs from their bills.

The willow's fears grew anew
Each day; the breath she drew
Became a dry, murmuring sigh,
Beseeching Zephyr for his aid
To make the hot summer fade
With cool air and cloudy shade
And some rain to ease her pain.
Soon God answered her prayer.

Our Hope

When we cry
In the wilderness,
Bitten by our loneliness,
Do You hear us?

Yes, yes, surely —
We presume we are blessed;
If we didn't believe so certainly,
How else would we be solaced!

Yet our fears,
Lurking behind our hopes,
Drown us in blinding tears,
Pulling us down the slippery slopes.

But we are sustained
By Your love and mercy.
This hope is firmly retained
In our breast as a prophecy.

Our Occupation

We open windows to let in the light
We light electric candles to see in the night
We go to the church to expiate our sin
We open our hearts to let others in
We knock on doors, wanting to be let in
We make a promise and keep it unbroken
We picture a world of peace and justice
We see necessity in this idea and practice
We respect life, liberty, and happiness
We work to remain in health and fitness
We don't like to remain static
We like all strains of art and music
We love playing and watching sports
We enjoy thrilling rides in cars and boats
We are kind to our cats and dogs
We are good at raising cows and hogs
We excel in science and technology
We have made great strides in cosmology

For all these virtues we make no apology
For we are Americans who love diversity

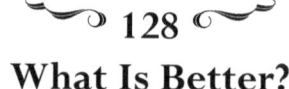

What Is Better?

Is it better to be a fool or a clever person?
Let's figure it out, dear son, and be done.

******

The fool knows little, but has some fun
Basking on a beach, loving earth and sun,
Sleeping under the stars, worrying none.

The clever one has no time for such kicks,
For he is too busy sharpening his tricks
To run down others with his gleeful smirks.

A real fool is eager to please everyone,
Ready to put all his belongings on lease
To pay for his friends' delinquent fees.

The clever one uses charm to inflict harm
In ways too cunning to raise any alarm
And by fake pleasantry to win and disarm.

The fool employs simpler ways to please:
His comic ignorance, innocence, and ease,
Which endear him to others in a breeze.

A clever guy uses others as a perfect tool
To advance his own mischievous plans,
Then subjects the helping hand to ridicule.

So, while the fool plays from spring to fall,
The clever make life a harsh winter for all.
Now, my son, who would you prefer to be?
Look at this paradox closely, and decide freely.

Be a Victor

Let us move forward
Without a backward look;
Mistakes made in the past
Must not hook or bind us
In the Gordian knots
That can't be untied,
Except by a novel thought,
As the great Alexander applied.

So let's move ahead and join
The victors who don't get bogged
In the swampy theaters
Where old alligators of fear and doubt
Prevail, propagate, and regale,
Eating us from inside out.

Victors and victories
Fill the pages of history,
With wars fought to free or enslave;
But there are other battles too
That we fight every day,
Challenging our valor in another way.
These battles are fought in our hearts,
Where prowess alone is not enough;
But mastering the self is required,
For selflessness is the victor's ground,
And love and care his throne.

Selflessness

Yes, to be immune
To loss or gain,
Pleasure or pain,
Is seen by saints and sages
As an uplifting virtue
That shields us from sorrow.

Some construe this to mean
That we shouldn't on feelings lean
Or possess any sensitivity,
For these traits make us weak;
So let us be rather insensitive,
And indifference seek!

But a lack of feelings
For others' grim suffering,
Destitution, or disease
Also lends to more suffering
That noble hearts dread
Seeing or imposing.

For it destroys
Our faith in humanity,
And sorrows find no relief
As the unfeeling keep on
Selling with impunity
Their conscience to Grief.

These contrary views
Beg to be settled thus:
If moved by your gain or loss,
You are weak and selfish;
If moved by others' heavy cross,
You are strong and selfless.

Faith

"Too long to bondage Reason was consigned,
Chained by Religion, tyrant of the mind."
-Lucretious, *On the Nature of Things*

Some say they have seen the truth eternal,
Hidden in their hearts and vaguely supernal,
Through a reflection of the word paternal
That rapidly evolved into a faith fraternal.

Driven by a passion to remain united in a fold,
No one dares to question and break the hold
Of ideas that are hackneyed and definitely old,
Yet powerful enough to render judgment cold.

Each group and sect in its truth finds some rest
And considers it as the ultimate and the best;
In this conceit, they plunder, pillage, and test
The faith of another and stomp it into dust.

The civilized factions use a gentler approach:
They proselytize, preach, teach, and coach
To give up your belief and adopt their faith,
Promising everlasting love, life, and the wraith.

Like the frogs in a narrow well, they can't see
That there are waters much larger than a cup of tea,
Some deep 'n' clear, some rich in pearl as in the sea;
But, alas, all they can see is my, mine, and me!

Split Images

Shards of a broken mirror
Speak with many faces,
Each exhibiting its terror
Of the split-self it encases.

Similar is the fate of love
That can't keep its breath
In reaching the stars above,
And thus crashes to its death.

Pieces of a picture puzzle,
When put together aright,
May delight and dazzle us,
Yet their outlines do affright.

Stray remarks rearranged
Can be taken differently:
Bleakly by the estranged,
Brightly by the unchanged.

What I Fear

I dare not tell you
What I fear, earnestly,
For you may laugh at me;
But if it's sunny tomorrow,
I may feel differently.

I fear the wind may pick up
Tonight from the lee.
It will shake down
Many a flowering tree
For being closer to the sea.

It is the smell of salt and fish
That chokes the trees and me.
The wind is free and autocratic,
Lusting, gusting wildly
To denude a flowering tree.

The Truth

Truth is a goddess:
beautiful and sublime,
of many forms and functions,
existential and transcendental,
showing what is real and ethical:
veracity, faithfulness, and fidelity.

Truth can be too bitter or sweet;
she can lift you off your feet
or throw you on your face,
but in either case
she will make you wiser,

even richer, never a miser.
Truth may reveal her face
by God's grace,
but she is too difficult to find,
for she is not so kind
to each and every one,
seeking her with reverence none.

Truth lies hidden
in the caverns of mystery,
mind, matter, and shards of history,
awaiting love and labor to yield
the facts necessary to reveal
her true identity concealed.

Truth may want us to stay afloat
like a lotus on serene waters, and wait,
or plunge in a Promethean urge
to meet her at the subterranean gate,
just for a little wisdom to gain
that would lessen our existential pain.

Truth may sometimes clash
with her child called Civility,
causing hurt feelings – even animosity;
but one can't gag the truth
or exchange her for untruth,
as civility can't hide truth's luminosity.

We often refrain
from scratching the surface,
for fear of knowing the truth
about our beliefs, desires, and actions,
others' feelings, responses, and reactions,
and thus prefer to remain uncouth.

What I Want

I know what I want now and why,
On this earth and beyond the sky,
Conscious or unconscious I may lie
While alive, and even after I die.

Power, glory, or fame I don't need.
Riches or rewards aren't my mead.
On pure knowledge I want to feed.
From ego's hold I want to be freed.

Add one more thing to these gifts,
Dear God, give me love that uplifts,
Saving us from falling into icy drifts
Of wily indifference and deep rifts.

Fill me with sweet breath of love,
That I may on its wings soar above
The abyss of hate — a thirsting dove
Searching for You bough to bough.

I see You in every branch and leaf.
I see: You are central to each belief.
Every being and soul seeks relief.
So do I — from my existential grief.

So I beg for that kind of wisdom —
Suffused with love — seen seldom,
Which is needed for a soul's freedom
To secure a place in Your kingdom.

Being and Becoming

These countless spheres
Hanging out in space –
Some young, some old,
Some hot, some cold;
One of them a live planet blue,
Others give us no plausible clue.
But what purpose to their maker—
God or nature – do they serve?

Likewise, countless forms
Of life on this planet Earth,
Simple to most complex,
Their cells or muscles flex
And show cognitive intelligence
Ascending from molecule to man.
But I wonder why their maker—
God or nature – made it so happen?

Most believe God made the universe
For He felt lonely and lovelorn;
Others say it was nature's doing,
For natural laws keep on going.
These notions invoke some emotion
But fail to satisfy a simple question:
How can a self-sufficient God be lovelorn?
How would nature by itself be born?

This riddle is not easy to solve,
Unless all parties resolve
To bring a light of thought without blame
And see: the maker and the things made
May be one and the same;
For God may have created the universe
To discover and enjoy His own being,
Becoming many out of one truth or law.

The Two Paths

You have chosen
The path of love and devotion
— Bakhti-Yoga —
For your liberation[1],
Flying on the wings of a dove
Far above the path of knowledge
— Janana-Yoga —
Avoiding the serpent and the tree.

You follow the words
Of Krishna and Christ:
The promised life through love,
A simple path ensuring your tryst
With the personal God
Who redeems His devotee
By returning his love,
With grace, accordingly.

I try to seek Him
In His imminent form
Revealed before our eyes
In all the seasons, sounds, and seas,
In the leaves of grass and the galaxies.
For the path of knowledge (Janana)
Unites one with the Holy Spirit
Of Brahman[2], eternally.

Yes, spiritual knowledge
May lead us to the Transcendent,
But it is not possible for all.
The very few who try and succeed

---

1 Salvation, Moksha, Nirvana
2 Godhead; absolute truth, pure consciousness, and complete bliss.

Have truth and grace on their side
And find a place in the self of God.
But for those like you and me,
Let love our path to Him be.

You have accepted the world
As it is, by seeing and sorting
And by lovingly consorting
With samsara's[3] ebb and flow;
You freed your mind of its doubt
By choosing love over knowledge.
You're content with what you know,
But I have yet in this respect to grow.

3 The ever-changing world/universe

Longing

I keep rushing
Down the mountain
Like a thirsty stream
In search of the ocean
To quench my thirst
For perpetual motion.

I keep blowing
Through groves of trees
Like a fierce, whipping wind,
Searching for the fallen leaves
Of the tree of knowledge
That, for no reason, grieves.

I keep dashing
Like a hungry lion
To catch the fleeting prey,
But with no appetite today,
I let it run away,
For my mane has turned gray.

Now I ask God
For my deliverance
From this commotion
That keeps me on the run,
Serving no purpose or fun
Except pumping my emotion.

Whence I Come

I didn't come here on my own.
(It wasn't in my power to do so.)
You cast me from Yourself — as a stone
Thrown in a live dimension of space,
Requiring me now to find my place
With my free will to figure and find:
Whence I come, where must I go?

You are the king sitting on the hill;
I am the arrow shot from your bow.
It all started from Your own will,
So how come I am responsible
To find my way in a valley so low?
All I know is what I sense and feel:
Whence I come, there I want to go.

I know you like to dance and play,
To revel in your own manifestation;
And it pleases you to mold the clay
Around a soul to seek its destination,
Knowing well its natural inclination
To reach its home (You) with no delay;
Whence I come, there I must go.

So why have you sent me here
To struggle through a jungle of pain —
Sufferings of love and hate to endure?
What joy or knowledge is there to gain
In descending from mountain to plain?
Am I right? Or do I err or perjure?
Whence I come, there I shall go.

Belonging

For a long time I believed
The things I had acquired
With effort or ease –
For me to advance or shine
Or my ego to please –
Were really mine.

Then one day I woke up
From my deep sleep
In a new world of sunshine,
Where I could easily leap
And grasp the cup
I drink from, which is Thine.

Things I thought were mine –
My life, loves, and yearnings,
My career and earnings,
Things needed or unneeded,
Received often unimpeded –
Are actually Thine.

At times I asked for more,
As my desires kept a score.
You gave me what I needed;
Thy warning I never heeded.
Though it rang clear as a bell,
I couldn't its meaning tell.

Then it slowly came to me –
Not from any loss or sorrow,
But from a vision very fine –
That I am eternally Thine,

With all my belongings —
life, learning, and longings —
So grant me Thy love to acquire.
That's the only thing I require.

My Divine Friend

No measure of being can measure You.
No height is sufficient to reach You.
No depth is deep enough to fathom You.
No shape or form is perfect to match You.

I sense your presence always around me.
I sense your presence always within me.
But, alas! I can't see you with my eyes,
Nor, alas, can I reach you with my cries.

Why do you play these tricks with me?
Why do you first engage with me?
Why do you then disengage with me?
Why do you play hide-and-seek with me?

Is it because we are so different?
Is it because you are so indifferent?
Is it because you are too distant?
Or is it because we are one?

If you love me, indeed, as they say,
If you made me in your image, as they say,
If you want my adoration, as you command,
Help me know You better, I humbly demand.

You and Me

I am a vessel
Made of clay.
You fill me again and again
With your breath – to play.

In this way,
We have become one.
Like the tide and ocean,
Our union can't be undone.

Your presence,
Both far and near,
Ensures my existence,
Without any doubt or fear.

But for You I couldn't be;
Without creating me,
You wouldn't be happy.

Light Supreme

"Hail holy Light, offspring of Heav'n first born,
Or of the Eternal coeternal beam
May I express the unblamed? Since God is light."
-John Milton, Paradise Lost, Book 3

Oh! what can I do without You,
Who has hidden His countenance
Behind the sun and stars — not few
But all — imitating Your brilliance,

Making it difficult to understand
Who is who, and who the shaker
Of light in this universe grand?
Who the mover? Who the maker?

If it's true You are the source of light,
Then why are there so many stars
Bent on hiding You from my sight?
Could it be they are Your avatars?

If I knew, I would fly to You faster
Than light, on the wings of thought
(Painted in gold on white alabaster),
Fueled by poesy in my craving heart.

As I am waiting for this truth to dawn,
I breathe, eat, sleep, dream, and rise—
Just to remain alive — but withdraw,
Until I see You with my own eyes.

Dear God, illuminate me with a vision
Of Your real form and presence;
It would dispel my darkest confusion.
I can't do it without your guidance.

Grace and Karma

Man is lost without God's grace.
Love's loss nothing can replace.
Wealth and power have a place,
But loss of either is no disgrace

Grace is a gift of divine mercy,
Shown to those who err but remain
In God's far reaching eye still worthy.
The rest of us are bound to causality.

Cause and effect are linked eternally;
The law of karma governs inherently.
When deception is practiced indulgently,
Misfortune attends to it imminently.

The goodness you show never forego.
To bad feelings and actions say no.
The fair and foul times come and go;
They are just transitory in their flow.

Wait for your action's fruit to ripen,
For it will in its sweet time happen.
With learning let your mind sharpen;
With love in your heart, it'll brighten.

The air in a vessel may give us a sign
Of its separate existence from Thine,
You are in all, yet we bow in a shrine;
This illusion of duality we deem fine

God is not a subject among subjects.
God is not an object among objects.
The whole universe resides in Brahman[1].
As it manifests, a man-god resurrects,
But, in truth, only Brahman exists.

---

1 Supra-cosmic godhead, the imminent and transcendental principle of existence; absolute truth, pure consciousness, and complete bliss.

Brahman

My being was before my becoming.
In thee, O Brahman[1], all was dwelling,
Unmanifest, nirguna[2], formless,
Undifferentiated, in pure consciousness.
In truth and bliss existence was reveling.

Then love arose in cosmic splendor.
Self separated from the Supreme Self
As light from thunder;
Spirit entered the primordial matter
To enjoy Thy manifestation in wonder.

Nirguna became Saguna[3], the Isvara.[4]
Matter gave means of sense perception,
Ego and individuation without exception.
But my spirit was now caught in a vase;
Thus bound and limited, I lost my place.

My fall from heaven made me wander
From form to form, here and yonder,
To find my way home;
In cycles of birth and death I emerge
Again and again, only to submerge.

Submerge in the infinite ocean of bliss,
Eternal truth and pure consciousness –
Liberation, Moksha[5], Nirvana.
The homeward journey must now start;
My being must submerge in "Thou Art."

1 Supra-cosmic Godhead
2 Brahman without attributes
3 Brahman with attributes— personal God, Ishvara
4 God the Creator
5 Liberation from cycles of birth and death (Atman's merger with Brahman)

Atman[1]

I am the light of the sun and the stars
That illumines my way on this planet,
And through the sky into deep space
As I journey to my inner resting place.

I am the earth, the air, and the fire,
All the plants that drape this sphere,
All creatures of land, water, and air,
Respiring to keep the fire of life near.

I am the river, its ripples and flow,
Swelling the ocean – which too I am –
And the laden cloud of blessings grand
Falling as rain on the seas and land.

I am the moving dot of consciousness,
Expanding – so creating the universe,
With all its raw matter and motion,
Like a wave riding an infinite ocean.

I am the song, the singer, and the listener,
The melody flowing forth as Kala, the time.
I am the voice of silence, as one can tell;
I am closer to you than heaven or hell.

I am the truth of each subject and object.
I am the mind and the intellect that guide
One through the darkest period of night
To find true knowledge, bliss, and light.

---

1 Soul, the deepest self of man; a spark of Brahman, some equate Atman with Brahman

Star of Bethlehem

O Star of Bethlehem, lead me there,
Where a baby's breath filled the air,
Spreading light in the darkened cave
Of human mind – in order to save it.

Here God was born to toil and try
As a man, and to plant the seeds of love
In the arid lands and hearts that cry
Out for rain to wet them somehow.

My heart and mind are thirsting too
For the blest shower of such a rain
That makes the seeds of love to move
And grow into flowers without strain.

The son of man, who was born to die
And to rise again, fills me with awe;
I beg him to reside in my mind's eye,
For in him the miracle of God I saw.

Walking the talk under the blazing sun,
He showed how to be strong and kind
And to forgive those who have us undone;
For it's a sure way we can happiness find.

O Star of Bethlehem, lead me there:
Where truth and vision are quite clear,
Where the light of love shines on our path,
Purging our souls from greed and wrath.

Thank You

Thank you, dear God, for making me be
Of humankind, to see this world and find
Thy divine Lila[1] in space, time, and mind —
All, in adoration, to see, contained in Thee.

Though my time is short and brief,
This gives me no trouble, doubt, or grief;
Each moment of my life is richly filled,
As Thy love and grace keep me thrilled.

So why should I fear that my time is near?
I know deep in my soul You are there
To show me the way — then take me away,
As I awaken to your Maya's[2] incredible sway.

In animating this lump of Prakritic[3] clay,
Thy spark changed me from night into day;
There is nothing I want to have or save.
Oh God, I am thankful for the gift You gave.

Your precious gift of life enjoins us to see
The parts and purpose of all there can be,
From the tiny atom to the largest galaxy,
Primitive impulse to science and technology.

My deliverance, Moksha[4], will not easily come
Until my soul has completely Yours become.
Oh, could love and knowledge take me there!
But first: grace and devotion are needed here.

1 Divine play/activity; divine dispensation
2 Power by which the phenomenal world is created/manifested
3 Material cause of nature/world—in Shankhya philosophy
4 Attainment of liberation/salvation/nirvana

At the End of the Day

Oh! the day has ended
Sooner than I expected;
Now how can I complete
All the neglected tasks
That scream "incomplete."

The time to go has come.
I'll shed my clothes now,
Lighten my load somehow,
For I've to go on a journey.
Let my tasks incomplete be.

I can't keep Him waiting,
For there is a price to pay,
Far greater than to meet
The unmet obligations that lay
Golden traps under my feet.

He knows why I failed
To carry my cross to Calvary.
He knows how I was assailed
By doubt and attendant strife;
But I have His word of afterlife.

My Prayer

I rarely go to a temple, church, or a shrine,
But I love Thee dearly, and also pine.
So please tell me:
When and where shall I offer
My prayers to Thee,
O God Supreme?

At dawn!

When the sun and the birds
Are already up,
In joyous communion with Thee,
Offering wreathes of light and melody,
Reminding me
Of my insufficiency in words and voice
To praise Thee!

At dusk!

When thoughtful men and women,
With their uplifted eye,
Pray for you to appear in the starry sky,
The evening air and love that for
You sigh; My vision gets blurred
By tears of joy,
Choking my voice and word.

Day and night!

Dear God, I have heard
You are merciful and kind
To all — in keeping with Your word —
Even to those who are dumb and blind.
So, accept my prayers I silently make
Everywhere, all the time.

INDEX

END of the Manuscript